THREE GREEK TRAGEDIES
IN TRANSLATION

THE UNIVERSITY OF CHICAGO PRESS
CHICAGO, ILLINOIS

✳

THE BAKER & TAYLOR COMPANY
NEW YORK

THE CAMBRIDGE UNIVERSITY PRESS
LONDON

THREE
GREEK TRAGEDIES IN
TRANSLATION

❧

DAVID GRENE
The University of Chicago

THE UNIVERSITY OF CHICAGO PRESS
CHICAGO · ILLINOIS

To

MY FATHER AND MOTHER

PREFACE

THIS book is intended for two kinds of readers: first, for the students who study Greek tragedy in translation either in courses specifically devoted to that subject or in general drama courses and, secondly, for people outside universities who care to find out what a Greek tragedy is like. I am keenly aware of the shortcomings of the translations: few who have not tried their hands at the job of rendering into English a Greek play can have any idea how difficult it is. It should, it seems to me, be rendered in verse, for the verse medium in any language imposes certain restrictions which vitally affect the character of the whole piece and must be represented by a similar kind of restriction in the language of the translator. But English has no verse medium which exactly reproduces the Greek iambic trimeter. The latter's distinguishing characteristic is a flexibility which enables it to be magnificent without pomposity and simple without falling into the inane. English blank verse can be magnificent; but it is extremely difficult, if not impossible, to prevent its falling into a helpless inanity when it is written to express the very simplest effects of dramaturgy. A good deal of such material in the Elizabethan and Jacobean dramatists is rendered in prose. When certain of them, notably Massinger, try to write regular blank verse for the simplest dramaturgical needs—for the "open the door" and "let him come in" and so on of the play—they are flat and bad. And when in our own time Maxwell Anderson, aware of this difficulty, tried to solve it by loosening up his blank-verse structure until it appeared to be neither verse nor prose, the effect of formalism and spontaneity—the hallmark of this kind of material in Greek drama—was still not achieved. Some of such passages in these three Greek tragedies I have rendered in prose. Some are in verse, whose simplicity is so excessive that I fear it is often prosy. But, as a rule, I have sought rather to err on the side of a prosaic simplicity than on that of an affected and pseudo-poetic jargon, which is the besetting fault of most nineteenth-century English translations. Furthermore, I have attempted honestly to render the Greek into its corresponding English terms without the infusion of the spice of "faery lands forlorn," which is the worst feature of Professor Murray's popular versions.

The choric parts of the plays were written in the original in a free, if formalized, kind of verse which seemed to me best represented in English by a simple free-verse form. Sometimes the rendering is effective, I think; sometimes I cannot reproduce the musical effect of the original without rhyme, which is a dangerous expedient, for the fixity of the musical pattern is too inflexible for the Greek. The various experimentalist translations of Greek plays in the past decade—the excellent versions of Louis MacNeice, Dudley Fitts and Robert Fitzgerald, George Thomson, and Edith Hamilton—are happiest, in my opinion, when they do not render the Chorus predominantly in rhyme.

Two of the particular introductions appeared originally in a slightly different form in *Classical Philology*, and my thanks are due to the editors of that journal for permission to reproduce them here. The general introduction is a condensation of a series of lectures given by me in the Humanities Survey Course at the University of Chicago.

To the various classes of my students, on whom the raw material has been tried, I owe far more than they know or I can acknowledge.

D. G.

TABLE OF CONTENTS

* * *

GENERAL INTRODUCTION

THERE is perhaps nothing more characteristic of the theater of any period than the conventions which it accepts. The aggregate of these conventions constitutes what we choose to call the *form* of a given theater, as opposed to the plot, which is regarded as the *matter* of the plays. And it is in the form rather than in the matter, if we may use these rather equivocal terms in the sense defined, that the major differences reside between one kind of drama and another: it is in virtue of a difference in form rather than in subject matter that we pronounce as different kinds of theater, say, Aeschylus' *Oresteia*, Cocteau's *Machine infernale*, and Eugene O'Neill's *Mourning Becomes Electra*. One can further illuminate the relative importance of form and matter in the theater by showing that there seems to be little difference, basically, between the *plots* of tragedy and those of comedy. *Othello* with another kind of interpretation of a lighter sort becomes the plot of *The Country Wife*. The differences between any of the periods of tragic theater or between tragedy and comedy are differences created not by the nature of the subject matter but by the spirit in which an audience receives what is said on the stage and in particular on the degree of realism the audience is accustomed to in such a performance. But, in considering the spirit in which the audience receives the dramatist's work and the degree of realism to which theatergoing people are accustomed, we are in fact dealing with the conventions of that theater.

As to the basic subject matter of tragedy, he would be a bold man who would think that he could circumscribe it in a sentence or two. But it is plain to anyone who knows more than a few different kinds of theater, or different periods of the same theater, that it has a uniformity which the varying conventions lack. Apparently, tragedy always centers in some elemental conflict between man and a destiny he can-

1

not master. At one time that conflict may be interpreted as man's defeat through an error which is moral, which he would have avoided had he been wiser or more virtuous. At another time it may be the defeat of man through forces so arbitrary and so outside his control that in the heroic bearing of his defeat we, who are men as well as he, see the marks of victory. At still another time the defeat of man may be an unrelieved sorrow with, at best, the text "as flies to wanton boys, are we to the gods, they kill us for their sport." But there seems to be little great or deep variation of this tragic theme, wherever we look in the theater of the Western world from Aeschylus to O'Neill. And, whether the audience is predominantly interested in the exposition of great truths in man's relation with man, as the Greeks for the most part were, or with exciting tales of adventure, of blood and murder, as the Elizabethans were, or with the new criticism of what seemed profound social and religious sanctions, as late nineteenth-century Europe was, the stuff of tragedy remains the same. The dramatist is the child of his age in that, if he is a great dramatist, he will write in the way that his age wants him to write; but some deeper obligation of his nature forces him to write of the tragic theme which all his predecessors have handled too. So, if we wish to understand any particular period of drama, what we must do is to peel off the conventions which are alien to our own period, until we have realized the reason for them and can accept them, intellectually, as their contemporary audiences accepted them instinctively. It is in this way that we can come to the core of the tragedy, which is always the same. It is in this way that we may have some real understanding on which to set side by side *Prometheus*, *Lear*, and *Ghosts*.

"The conventions which an audience accepts and is accustomed to" is a loose phrase and needs further definition. In its simplest sense, of course, it is the particular form, the mold into which the dramatist's story is poured. It is a kind of distortion of his material, employed willingly or unwillingly by the artist, either traditionally or as the result of a personal and individual preference. It may be some element of reality left out, as in the case of the Byzantine painters, who painted in only two, rather than three, dimensions. In such a case the convention is purely an aesthetic one; and by "aesthetic" I mean the quality in a work of art which enables people to understand it as a work of art. The contemporaries of the Byzantine painters did not believe that they saw the ordinary people of this world two-dimensionally, but they accepted the convention according to which objects were so represented because, they would have told you, that is the way the painter works. There would have appeared to such Byzantine critics no natural reason for claiming that the painter should imitate the ordinary world more exactly.

The Greek Chorus is such a purely aesthetic convention, in that this band of fifteen old men or women friends of the heroine or captives of war is taken to represent the average sentiment of the average man or woman in opposition to the extraordinary man or woman who is the center of the play. So in the Elizabethan theater is the aside a convention, for it assumes that we will accept the revelation of the sentiments of a character on the stage as possible, where in the ordinary circumstances of life neither their vocal exposition nor even their verbal formulation would seem reasonable. So in the theater of Ibsen is the three-sided room a convention of the aesthetic kind. We assume that we are allowed to see within each room, which in ordinary life would possess a fourth wall to exclude the onlooker.

But there is another kind of convention which may be defined as the representation of some unrealistic factor in a given situation, which the audience, or at least a large part of it, can be brought to accept as a representation of the real world. This commands neither exactly the credence with which the dramatist's artistry invests improbable "natural" things nor the willing acceptance which the blatantly artificial convention receives in virtue of a willing agreement between author and audience. Such a convention, which with apologies I shall call a "psychological convention" to distinguish it from the aesthetic variety,

is directed just at the point where the audience' belief ends
and its disbelief has not yet quite asserted itself. Some examples may make this clearer than further explanation.
The Ghost in the Elizabethan theater is not exactly an
unreality, the presence of which has been tacitly accepted by
the audience in its willing suspension of disbelief. While I
am confident that many of the Elizabethan theatergoers
were suspicious of the occurrence of ghosts and witches, I
am equally confident that a certain section of the Elizabethan audience would have received Hamlet's father with
complete credulity. This is a case in which the dramatist
uses for dramatic purposes a belief which his audience finds
it relatively easy to accept *almost* on realistic grounds and
not, as in the case of the Chorus, where the audience out of
tradition is willing to let the dramatist dictate to them a
patently unrealistic way of representing a realistic fact. And
in an Ibsen play the extraordinary compression and ac-
celerated tempo of the action are only noted, if noted at all,
by a small part of the audience. So skilfully does the author
do his task that most of those who see the play involuntarily
believe that such a conveniently dramatic pace prevails in
the conditions of real life, rather as many of the Elizabethans accepted the ghost as a likely factor in ordinary life.
In the Greek theater the connection of the legend, which is
treated by the dramatist, with historical or archeological
facts is a convention of a similar kind. Certainly, many who
went to the Dionysiac theater did not believe that the story
of Hippolytus, as Euripides tells it, was the occasion of the
foundation of the worship of Hippolytus in Athens. But
many of them certainly did, or at least accepted it as a
likely story and in a different mood from that in which they
accepted the presence of the Chorus on the stage. Sometimes, too, what once constituted a convention of the second
or psychological kind may later become a convention of the
first or aesthetic kind. For instance, in present-day perform-
ances of *Hamlet* the Ghost is not accepted as many of the
Elizabethans accepted him. He has become for us an aes-

thetic convention similar to the aside which the Elizabethans accepted as an aesthetic convention.

To study the three plays which I have selected from the point of view of the psychological convention would mean a burrowing into the historical factors in the development of the Greek stage and in the origin of each play. Instead of doing this, I intend to draw an arbitrary line around the particular conventions governing methods of dramatic presentation, and that will virtually restrict me to consideration of what I have referred to as the purely aesthetic conventions. The three chief are the Chorus, the verse, and the myth-plot.

THE CHORUS

In general the Chorus is a response to the need of the play for some intermediary between the actors and the audience. Such a purpose is served in the Chinese play by the reader and in the modern radio play by the announcer. But behind this satisfaction of an obvious dramaturgical need stands a subtler intention, which is closely connected with the very existence of histrionic display. It is scarcely possible to realize the extraordinary (and in some sense the events of a tragedy are always extraordinary) without an immediate comparison with the ordinary and average, either in character or in action. So sometimes, and particularly at crucial moments in tragedy when the tension is greatest, it is expedient to have the Chorus voice the most obvious and ordinary sentiments in the most obvious and banal way. For by this means we cast out the imp of disbelief and denigration which lives somewhere in every spectator, asserting that the world is not what the dramatist says it is or that the tragedy is an unnecessary fuss about nothing. In such instances the Chorus is so ordinary, so matter of fact, and so dully imperceptive that, recognizing the disbelieving or uncomprehending part of ourselves, we reject it. So our rational and ordinary selves are drained away, as it were, leaving us in the condition of mild hypnosis needed by the dramatist to tell us what he has to tell us. It is very interesting to notice how Shakespeare uses some of his comic characters in just such a choric function in the great tragedies. The gravedigger's cheerful cynicism concerning the dead and their capacity for rotting is the confession of that part of us least sympathetic with Hamlet's subtle whimsicalities. The scene is the supreme example of the ironic contrast between the comedy and the tragedy of man's ignominy. But the gravedigger's statement of our position is so indifferent to the humanity common to himself and the corpse that, while we laugh, we are repelled and draw closer to Hamlet. In the *Prometheus* of Aeschylus, when Io quits the scene (the tortured cow-maiden, hounded over the paths of the world because of Hera's jealousy and Zeus's love), the Chorus observes that this is an illustration of the unwisdom of marrying above your station. Here again, as in the *Hamlet* passage, there is a reduction of a tragic situation to its lowest possible terms in order that the expression by such terms may banish the part of us that remains obdurately unawakened or cynical in the face of the dramatist's magic. Besides, in this last play the Chorus has the peculiarly difficult task of acting as medium between divine and human beings. We are constantly in danger—or at least a part of each of us is in danger—of protesting that the doings of gods do not concern us, that they are different from us, and that we cannot understand their predicament. The Chorus helps, on all these counts. It reduces the divine tragedy of Io and Zeus to a very common human story and thus links our understanding of the human to an understanding of the divine situation; at the same time, by the obvious banality of the comment, it prevents us, even unconsciously, from making that comment when we think of the situation as a human situation.

It is noticeable that Greek plays often end on a very much lower and duller note than the climax of the tragedy which immediately precedes the end. And many of the Shakespearean tragedies exhibit an exactly similar feature. The end of *Hamlet* is not "The rest is silence" but Fortinbras's speech. The end of *Othello* is not "I took by the throat the circumcised dog And smote him thus" but the speech of

Lodovico, full of routine details of the final settlement of the episode and the future disposition of Cyprus. This slackening of the tension is a means of making us understand the meaning of the tragedy. When the extraordinary events have run their course, there must be some assurance that the world goes on as usual, so that we may understand how very extraordinary the events were. Certainly, we know that Fortinbras will not be a king such as Hamlet might have been, as surely as we know that Fortinbras is not a prince such as Hamlet was. A similar function is often discharged in Greek tragedy by the Chorus. For instance, the judgment of the Chorus on Hippolytus' tragedy, with all its divine cruelty, with the stupidity and treachery and passion of its human actors, is comfortably blanketed in the generalizations about the unexpected which God brings to pass.

Over and above this intellectual realization of the ordinary as opposed to the extraordinary there is the quality of Chorus and choric parts, which conventionally represent reality. The bit of Chorus at the end of *Hippolytus*, the lines of Fortinbras at the end of *Hamlet*, are close conventional representations of life as it exists. In real life the scene does not end in "the rest is silence" but with the babbling of fools, as Synge has it, or more often with the pointless generalizations of worthy but relatively unconcerned people. The intense part of the play's plot is played within the frame of the Chorus. They are in the play what the funeral ceremonies and the conventional words of sympathy are to the friends of the dead man in the world outside the theater.

It would obviously be a mistake to think that the Chorus in Greek tragedy or the choric characters in Shakespeare were conceived from the beginning as an aesthetic instrument and perfected with that in mind. Actually, of course, both the Greek Chorus and the comic characters, which are most frequently the Shakespearean chorus, originate historically in something which has nothing whatever to do with aesthetics. The Chorus was the very beginning of the Greek drama—a band of persons who sang a song together in honor of some god or hero. It is only later that one of the

Chorus detaches himself from the rest and holds conversation with the rest. This is the beginning of the actor and Chorus relation. Now it would have been perfectly possible to regard the Chorus as a very grave impediment to the development of the drama, since in any kind of drama which makes clear advances toward realism the unexplained presence of twelve or fifteen persons not directly concerned in the plot is a constant problem. But the Greeks deliberately took the Chorus—this historical accident which had been foisted on them—and shaped it for the dramatic purpose of representing the ordinary man or woman within the play. Similarly, Shakespeare had wished off on him the funnyman as a necessary part of the play, designed to keep the groundlings in the audience attentive. It would have been quite conceivable that he should have decided that the comic side of the thing was an inappropriate nuisance and have done his best to differentiate it sharply from the rest of the piece and perhaps have left the writing of the comic parts to others. That, in fact, is probably what Marlowe did. But Shakespeare, instead, made of his disadvantage a magnificent aesthetic advantage, whereby he not only pleased the groundlings but even harmonized the comic with the tragic elements in his play in a relation designed to pass the test of the most judicious critic. Quite similar is the case of the Elizabethan want of scenery and the male impersonation of female parts and, in the Greek theater, the restriction of plot to a few myths. In every instance a historical accident of at least a neutral and sometimes an extremely unfavorable character for the theater is by artistic ingenuity wrested into a great advantage. It would almost seem as if the most effective works of art, in the theater at least, grow out of a struggle with historical factors unfavorable materially and intellectually, when the playwright makes a deliberate attempt to mold them into the service of a contemporary artistic creation.

Turning now from the general theory of the relationship of Chorus to players and of both to the audience, it is possible to work out roughly four main practical uses to which the Greek dramatists put the Chorus in their tragedies.

1. *As an actor in the drama of an importance comparable with the main character.*—This is, of course, the position originally occupied by the Chorus before the actors stole the interest of the spectators. The earliest Aeschylean play, *The Suppliants*, is little more than a succession of choric odes broken up at infrequent intervals by dialogue. There is virtually no plot and almost no dramatic tension. Even in this, the earliest stage of the Greek tragedy after it can be formally recognized as tragedy rather than as a mere act of choric worship, the Chorus is already a different sort of actor from the main characters. It is not the Chorus which makes the drastic decisions on which depends such dramatic excitement as the play possesses. The Chorus is already at most a generalized or typical figure in contrast with the individual actors. It is interesting to notice that this, the primitive function of the Chorus, continues throughout the life of Greek tragedy. This earliest play we possess—*The Suppliants* of Aeschylus—and one of the latest of Euripides—the *Bacchae*—are called after the Chorus, and in both of them the Chorus is of major importance.

2. *To create a certain emotional atmosphere necessary for the dramatic effect of the play.*—This can be done by a lyrical re-statement of the situation already sketched in the dialogue, as in the second Chorus of the *Agamemnon* and the *Helen* Chorus. These Choruses are also sometimes resumptive, but always with a bearing on the emotional color of the situation: for instance, the first long Chorus of the *Oedipus* with its account of the plague. Or the Chorus may have the lyrical detachment from the main body of the play necessary to carry the weight of the *sententiae* dear to the Greek heart. In such cases the choric parts become the statement in universal terms of the proposition already enunciated in particular and material terms by the action of the play. In such cases it nearly always quotes mythological backing for such generalizations as it permits itself.

3. *A narrative of antecedent events necessary for an understanding*

of the plot.—For instance, the first Chorus in the *Hippolytus*, when the women tell of Phaedra's illness. Or in the *Agamemnon* the first Chorus gives us a complete picture of the campaign at Troy and the series of events leading up to Iphigeneia's death. This is really essential in order to understand Agamemnon's character and Clytemnestra's feelings toward him. Without this useful medium, both ancient and modern dramatists are at a loss as to how to convey information which it is natural to presuppose known to all the actors in the drama, which must yet be conveyed to the audience that is watching the progress of the play. This need has led in the Elizabethan playwrights to an interminable series of tattling servants and elsewhere to the introduction of unnecessary strangers, who are there solely to listen to an exposition of events with which all the actors in them must be already familiar.[1] When Aeschylus does not avail himself of the chorus in this capacity, he has recourse to a somewhat clumsy device in the *Prometheus*, where Prometheus tells his story to the Oceanids, then tells them his fate in the years to come, tell them Io's past wanderings as proof of his craft, and gets Io to tell them more. The entire drama moves within the framework of slightly ludicrous confidences.

4. *Finally, the Chorus is used by the dramatist as an expression of his own sentiments and opinions.*—For this purpose he undoubtedly utilizes the characters as well, just as a modern dramatist would do, but there were obvious advantages in the Chorus medium, since the members of the Chorus, except in the one or two plays I have already mentioned, had no strong dramatic character to sustain, and hence the extra-dramatic opinions of the author were most fittingly put into their mouth. An instance is *Hippolytus:*

> The care of God for us is a great thing
> if a man believe it at heart.

VERSE

Poetic drama is a matter partly of diction and partly of a musical verse convention. The tragedies of Sophocles and

[1] For instance, the modern stage version of *Wuthering Heights*.

Euripides and the recent poetic tragedy of Yeats, Synge, Eliot, and Auden have in common a spoken diction, but a spoken diction heightened by the poetic conception. The same holds of the later Shakespearean tragedies. What is artificial in them is not the diction but the musical pattern of the blank-verse line. Aeschylus, however, transcends the limits of ordinary speech, and at its best his diction has the grandeur of Isaiah and the dramatic beauty of Marlowe. At its worst it is perilously near bombast—as Aristophanes saw, though with appreciation even of heroic bombast, and as Euripides saw without any sympathy. The diction of Sophocles and Euripides is really a conventionalized form of the spoken language, purified of slang but instinct with life. Actually, the more complete acceptance of the spoken dialect of the streets does not carry with it greater realism, simply because in modern life the radio, the cinema, and the press have produced a language on men's lips which is a succession of meaningless clichés in ordinary conversation and of dumbness or inarticulacy in moments of emotion. Few of the words or the expressions are their own, and they have a natural want of interest in the origins or visual connections of this readymade speech.

Apart from the choice of words, the poet who writes drama is forced sooner or later to decide on what lyrical level he can work without sacrificing his dramatic effects. For instance, despite Dryden's gallant fight for its maintenance and the occasional success of plays like *Richard II*, a rhymed couplet is apparently too lyrical for our English-speaking stage. The musical pattern is too constant and too strongly marked, and we cannot think of the whole speech but only of the individual couplets, for the tinkling of the endings and the resonance of the beats. Rhyme can be used, however, at intervals for heightening the color of a scene or an emotional moment and for such purposes is extremely effective. The Greek tragic convention served them well here. The Choruses are an emotional commentary on the piece, and the conventionalized Doric dialect in which they were written from time immemorial helped to heighten the

contrast with the rest of the dialogue, thus producing a sepa-
ration that avoids injury to the dramatic tone of the rest.
But in studying Greek drama, or any other highly conventionalized poetic theater, we must observe clearly, first, the
limits to expression which the employment of a verse medium imposes and, second, the character it stamps on the
spirit of the whole.

Whether or not Housman is right when he says that
there is no theme or mood too lofty for prose or too lowly for
verse, his judgment can be followed in dramatic verse only
with the greatest difficulty. Even the small details which
give the animation of real life are moderately difficult.
When Dryden writes, "One would think that 'unlock the
door' was a thing as vulgar as any can be spoken and yet
Seneca can make it sound high and lofty in his Latin,
reserate clausos regii postes laris," he is guilty of an absurdity as
egregious as the famous

> Holla, ye pampered jades of Asia!
> What, can ye draw but twenty miles a day?

This kind of bombast is not uncommon amid the glittering
golden beauty of Aeschylus. But Euripides, whose method
was the exact opposite of that of Aeschylus—for he puts his
commonplace details as naked and unadorned as a grocer
ticketing his goods—comes in for Aristophanes' censures in
the *Frogs* on the same score (980). The practical details,
which obtrude themselves as the dramaturgical necessities,
are always in danger from our critical faculties, which find
in the opposition of the triviality of content and the weighti-
ness of form a source of ludicrous comment.

But the main difficulty is in the conveyance of certain
complex moods. Poetic drama is in the main the treatment
of simple emotions: love, joy, jealousy, hate—but all in their
simplest form. The profundity of the dramatist consists in
impregnating the purely personal and simple emotion of the
character with that flavor of universality, the suggestion of
the unsaid, that gives the whole speech a value above its
dramaturgical significance. But when the speech must be

complex even in its relation to the person who utters it, the verse convention makes the dramatist's task a hard one. This is particularly true if the mood is not one of tension or of great dignity, if it is not "heroical" as the seventeenth century would call it. Shakespeare has been able to render this mood once or twice in his verse passages, notably once or twice in *Hamlet*, but it is extremely rare everywhere else. It may be said at once that it is unknown in Greek tragedy. For so are the elaborate introspective psychological investigations which are the background of such a mood. And that brings me to the second point of which I wanted to treat: that poetic drama implies a certain character in the spirit of the whole play and that this character is especially noticeable in the Greek tragedies.

The general trend of the realist drama is toward the ever minuter analysis of the emotions and character of the individual. The modern drama, having abandoned the poetic fire of its predecessors and being far too self-conscious to give overt expression to wisdom, feeling, or excitement in any perfected form, has been driven in the direction of an exclusive emphasis on either plot or character. Hence the modern "thriller" play or the psychological "static" play. The Greek, on the other hand, is interested primarily in the description of an emotion rather than a man, a moment rather than the texture of many moments that make up a life, the dramatic impact of a situation on the persons concerned in it rather than the situation with regard to their whole background. This has been put extraordinarily well by W. B. Yeats:

In poetical drama there is, it is held, an antithesis between character and lyric poetry, for lyric poetry—however much it may move you when you read out of a book—can, as the critics think, but encumber the action. Yet when we go back a few centuries, and enter the great periods of drama, character grows less and sometimes disappears and there is much lyric feeling, and at times a lyric measure will be wrought into the dialogue, a flowing measure that had well befitted music, or that more lumbering one of the sonnet. Suddenly it strikes us that character is continuously present in Comedy alone, and that there is much tragedy, that of

Corneille, Racine, that of Greece and Rome, where its place was taken by passions and motives, one person being jealous, another full of love or remorse or pride or anger. In writers of tragicomedy (and Shakespeare is always a writer of tragicomedy), there is indeed character, but we notice that it is in the moments of comedy that character is defined, in Hamlet's gaiety let us say. . . . . Nor does character ever attain the complete definition in these lamps ready for the taper, no matter how circumstantial and gradual the opening of events, as it does in Falstaff who has no passionate purpose to fulfil. . . . . Tragedy must always be a drowning of the dykes that separate man from man: it is upon these dykes that comedy keeps house. . . . . We may not find either mood in its purity, but in mainly tragic art one distinguishes devices to exclude or lessen character, to diminish the power of that daily mood, to cheat and blind its too clear perception. If the real world is not altogether rejected, it is but touched here and there and into the places we have left empty we summon rhythm, balance, pattern, images that remind us of vast passions, the vagueness of past times, all the chimaeras that haunt the edge of the trance; and if we are painters we shall express personal emotions through ideal form, a symbolism handled by the generations, a mask from whose eyes the disembodied looks, a style that remembers many masters, that it may escape contemporary suggestion: or we shall leave out some element of reality as in Byzantine painting, where there is no mass, nothing in relief, and so it is that in the supreme moment of tragic art there comes upon one that strange sensation as though the hair of one's head stood up. . . . . Tragic art, passionate art, the drowner of dykes, the confounder of the understanding moves us by setting us to reverie, by alluring us almost to the intensity of a trance. The persons on the stage greaten until they are humanity itself. We feel our minds expand convulsively or spread out slowly like some moon-brightened, image-crowded sea. That which is before our eyes perpetually vanishes and returns again in the midst of the excitement it creates, and the more enthralling it is the more do we forget it.[2]

MYTH-PLOT

Finally, there is the restriction on plot in the Greek tragedies. Aristotle in the *Poetics* discusses the reasons for the

[2] W. B. Yeats, *The Cutting of an Agate* (Macmillan, 1912), pp. 199 ff. By permission of the publishers.

use of the fixed-myth cycle, stating that in the stories of certain historical persons and their families are found in their most significant form the tragic happenings which condition tragic emotion and, secondly, that "what convinces us is the possible: now whereas we are not yet sure as to the possibility of that which has not happened, that which has happened is manifestly possible, else it would never have come to pass."

Of these two grounds, the first does not appear entirely convincing. It is surely possible that the contemporary history of Greece or the domestic life of their own time would have furnished the Greek dramatists with material as satisfactory as that of the legends. The second reason given by Aristotle is extremely important, once it is understood in reference to its Greek setting. The Greek myths would be the first imaginative meat of every Greek child. The form of the familiar myth drove home the poet's message with additional emotional conviction. Today, unluckily, we have almost no set of folk stories in any nation that have the same emotional appeal for the community as a whole. Because the different levels of education have severed us and mostly because of the enormous scale of the modern state, no dramatist can find a mold into which to cast his proposition, no story to which all will feel the emotional response awakened by memories of childhood. The nearest thing we have are some fairy stories, but they have, unfortunately, always been fairy stories for us, and when we grew older they ceased to be anything except the remnants of tales that amused us in childhood. But, for the Greeks, Heracles and Helen and their tragedies are real because they are folk memories, not the creations of folk imagination. We have divorced history from legend; they had not. Our folk stories are from the world of escape fantasy; theirs were, for the most part at least, realistic and firm. The anthropomorphism of their gods and their all-too-human lapses permitted the legends to retain their emotional validity.

This explains the use of the traditional names for the tragedies, and the traditional outlines for the plot. Within the not inelastic framework of the legend the dramatist could create. There was at least one play in which plot and characters were entirely invented: the *Anthus* of Agathon. But the precedent was not followed, and the dramatists appear to have stuck resolutely to the two or three best-known stories, like the legend of the House of Atreus or that of Oedipus and the Seven against Thebes or the Heracles cycle. Aristotle declares that even the framework of these plots would be known to only a small number among the audience; but that seems hardly likely. The situation must, in fact, have been similar to that in Ireland, where the stories of the Irish heroic ages are widely diffused in various forms throughout the countryside and, consequently, there is no absolute, rigid certainty of knowledge to be obtained about any of them. Frequently the Greek dramatist used a little-known variation of a legend found in the work of some previous lyric poet or bard. For instance, Euripides' *Helen* is based on the tale as told by Stesichorus. But it is still in its general outline the familiar story. This is psychologically an excellent opportunity for the dramatist, for the essence of a play does not lie in surprise. While we almost all can read thrillers and maintain the tension and genuine expectancy until the end, there are very few thriller plays whose outcome is not obvious after the first act. After that, if it is a good thriller, the dramatist maintains interest by the definitely dramatic emotion of making us wait to see in what form the already known event will take place. This was precisely the mental attitude of a Greek audience when they heard that they were going to see a play about the homecoming of Agamemnon. They knew that Agamemnon must be murdered by Clytemnestra, that Orestes must kill his mother and ultimately be haunted by the Furies for his deed, but they did not know in what particular form the Attic dramatist was going to use this sequence of events or what moral color would be put upon them. For a convincing indication of the different structures which can be built out of the same bricks, you might read in succession the *Oresteia* of Aeschylus, the *Electra* of Sophocles, the *Electra* of Euripides, and *Mourning Becomes Electra* of Eugene O'Neill.

The historical or semihistorical background of the Greek tragedies enabled them to convey an artist's criticisms of the community with the necessary indirectness. Writing about contemporary themes becomes all too often a propagandist attack or a polemic. Apparently, we have to stand back and see the subject with some abstraction before we can make the criticism universal and artistic as distinct from journalistic. On this point Aristotle has telling observations to make (*Poetics* 1451*a*):

> From what we have said it will be seen that the poet's function is to describe, not the thing that has happened, but the kind of thing that might happen, according to the laws of probability or necessity. The historian and the poet do not differ in that the one writes in meter and the other without it—for it would be possible to put Herodotus into verse and he would be no less an historian whether in verse or not. No, the difference is that the historian tells the event as it happened, the other as it might happen. So poetry is a more philosophical and serious thing than history, for it tells of universals and history of singulars. Now the nature of the universal statement is concerned with what sort of thing may happen to be said or done by what sort of man, according to the laws of probability or necessity. At this poetry aims and fixes proper names on the characters. But history relates what Alcibiades actually did or experienced. . . . . And if he [the poet] should come to take a subject from actual history, he is none the less a poet for that. For some of the historical events that have taken place may well be such that they are of the order of the universal—of the things that might and could happen. And it is in his treatment of this aspect of them that he is a poet.

We have extant one play concerned with an actual historical occurrence: the *Persae* of Aeschylus; and we know of another that had an unhappy fate, *The Capture of Miletus* by Phrynicus. Euripides not infrequently wrote propagandist plays in which the direct criticism of contemporary events was very thinly veiled, indeed—for instance, *The Suppliants* and the *Heracleidae*. They are certainly not his happiest efforts. But in general the Greek dramatists clung resolutely to the doctrine later formulated by Aristotle: "to record rather that which could happen than that which actually happened."

AESCHYLUS: *PROMETHEUS BOUND*

INTRODUCTION

IN THE eighteenth century the critics knew what they thought about the *Prometheus* of Aeschylus and knew why they thought it. It was a bad play because the structure was episodic, the characters extravagant and improbable, the diction uncouth and wild. Their handbook of criticism was the *Poetics* of Aristotle, either directly or indirectly drawn upon. And it is plain that the Aeschylean play does not measure up to Aristotelian standards. Since the eighteenth-century critics believed that there was only one canon for drama, rooted in the principles of Aristotle, they quite reasonably judged the *Prometheus* a bad play. During the nineteenth century, with the Romantic revival and the breakdown of the so-called "classical" rules of the drama, the *Prometheus* was acclaimed by the critics as a great work of art. But they so acclaimed it entirely in terms of its theme or its poetry and in the same breath spoke of the greatness of Sophocles' *Oedipus*, Shakespeare's *Hamlet*, and Goethe's *Faust*. There was no effort to discover what was the nature of Aeschylus' dramatic method which set him so apart from Sophocles that the eighteenth-century critics had refused to recognize his merit. Nor did they sift the striking differences which exist between the *Prometheus* and any of the Shakespearean tragedies or *Faust*. They contented themselves with vague and not entirely satisfied references to the *Prometheus* as a study-drama rather than a play for the theater. Or they observed that the *Prometheus* was a magnificent tragedy but very static.

I have tried in this essay to explain what I believe to be the dramatic design in the *Prometheus*—a design as clearly defined as that of Sophocles in the *Oedipus*. Other problems incidental to the consideration of the *Prometheus*, such as the position of our play in the trilogy as a whole and the probable nature of the conclusion, have been omitted from the discussion. I have only assumed that the final issue is some form of compromise between Zeus and Prometheus. This inference seems to be justified by the crucial lines in the extant play (pp. 43 and 44), and in general by the conclusion of the somewhat similar problem in the *Oresteia*, when the old gods and the new are at last reconciled.

In the case of the plays of both Sophocles and Euripides, plot and character are closely combined. The evolution of the plot is indicative of the character of the persons involved, and the character of these persons is the conditioning force of the plot. That is to say, while accidents arbitrarily occurring may force Oedipus into a position where no action is possible for him other than that which he takes, yet Oedipus' character is decisive as the determinant of the form of his speeches under stress of these circumstances and the violence of his reaction to this or that calamity. Oedipus is doomed to kill his father and marry his mother. But it is because he is a strong, resolute, and determined man that his reactions are what they are, and his speeches manifest what Aristotle calls "moral preference" (*proairesis*). So character and plot are bound up together, and the play is the evolution of a gradual *anagnorisis* of Oedipus. His naturally vigorous temper and his helpless ignorance are the conditioning forces of the plot. But action is its mainspring, for it is through action that we see the gradual changes in Oedipus. In this, as in all his plays, Sophocles aims to bring out the dramatic implications of a particular story. The myth is given life by the accurate reconstruction of the characters in terms of fifth-century Greek reality. Thus incidentally Sophocles deals with political, social, and moral problems inherent in his dramatic situations. But the problems come up naturally, as part of the story, and their solution has no authoritative voice. I do not think that anyone could give a satisfactory account of Sophocles' theology or of Sophocles' beliefs on the nature of the state or the relative validity of state law and moral law. True, such questions are raised in the seven extant plays; but they are raised, it would seem, because

Sophocles' knowledge of men involved him in such problems when he dramatized the myth. He has no solutions.
There is hardly even particular sympathy or the reverse in
the wonderfully impartial weave of the drama. If the story
is truly reported, says the poet in effect, we must imagine the
men and the situations involved to have been something like
this.

In Euripides the interest is centered either in character or
in the intellectual implications of the myth. By means of the
Prologue and Epilogue he shortens and cuts the myth until
its compass is the one short action which is to constitute the
plot. Within this action the author sometimes extends the
part of some particular character and writes the play around
it—as in the *Electra*, or in the *Hippolytus*, where he makes
Phaedra the center of the play. Or else he will expand the
thought implicit in some single situation far beyond the general design of the story. A good instance is the lengthy treatment of the entire democracy versus tyranny theme in *The
Suppliants*.

In both these poets, action is all important. It is only
through action carefully constructed that Sophocles can
dramatize the myth and effect his intimate combination of
plot and character. It is only by action that Euripides can
bring out either his minute study of character or the particular
moral, political, or religious argument he wishes to illustrate.
In the case of both alike, the poet is bent on giving the myth
an individual life of its own each time it is reincarnated in a
play.

As distinct from Sophocles, or from Euripides in his
psychological plays, Aeschylus is a great self-conscious
teacher, one who has come to certain conclusions as to man's
destiny and the divine government of the cosmos. As distinct from Euripides' interest in a solutionless presentation
of intellectual problems, Aeschylus is concerned to give a
positive theology which he conceives as having universal significance. So the myth is for him the illustration of a great
permanent truth which he finds at the heart of man's ac-
tivity. His dramatic imagination seizes on such truths as are

most frequently a compromise between two opposites, and consequently the myths he uses most are those which tell of conflict on a cosmic scale and conflict ultimately laid by some concessions on the part of both combatants.[1] To make the myth universally significant, both characters and plot must correspond symbolically with characters and plot on one or more levels in addition to the myth in which they are imbedded. On each of these levels there is character solidly developed. Each has a little drama of its own. But it is a drama which does not evolve through the medium of action within the piece. It is displayed through prolonged exposition in narrative, each stage of the exposition making an advance on the preceding in completeness. While it is possible to understand each level of the symbolism entirely in terms of itself, it is enormously enhanced in significance when all the others are taken into account. The story chosen is usually simple and uncomplicated, since it is nearly impossible to find a complicated story which can be significant on many levels at once.

The most striking difference, formally, between the Aeschylean drama and dramas subject to the Aristotelian criticism centers in their treatment of probability. Probability is the means whereby every dramatist induces that willing suspension of disbelief which is the prerequisite for the play. According to the Aristotelian criticism, probability is constructed almost entirely in terms of the play itself. That is to say, the probability of any incident in the play, of this or that trait which is important in the working-out of the character, must be solved in terms of the play itself. The dramatist may admit of many improbabilities in the situation assumed when the play opens; but, once it opens, the train of

[1] These generalizations on Aeschylus' dramatic method are not intended to be a complete statement. In their entirety they apply only, I think, to the *Prometheus*. The *Oresteia* is a curious combination of the kind of action-drama written by Sophocles and Euripides and the characteristically Aeschylean symbolic play. But hardly any of the plays of Aeschylus seem to me free of an allegorical meaning in which every dramatic symbol does duty twice or three times on different levels of significance.

causation must be clear in terms of the given situation. Coincidences are justifiable in limited number and even some improbable coincidences because, as Agathon says (*Poetics* 1456*a*), it is probable that some improbable things may happen. It is plain, however, that there is over and above this a probability which has its roots in the common experience of humanity. Absolute shifts from extreme hostility to extreme friendliness tend to break the force of the drama. In fact, the probability of the action is rooted in the conditions stated by the dramatist at the beginning, but the probability of the character is almost altogether rooted in the common experience of man.

In the Aeschylean symbolic play, like *Prometheus*, the probability is not in the action or the conditions the dramatist has stated for us before the play commences. It consists in setting forth a very simple story, one which comes from a common stock of mythological stories known to almost all, and fusing this with a number of other patterns known to almost all. Everybody in Greece knew the legend of the Titan who stole fire from heaven to give it to man. But everybody in Greece also knew the story of Peisistratus, the tyrant of Athens, or Lygdamis, the tyrant of Naxos, or Polycrates, the tyrant of Samos. They knew the kind of outrage citizens had suffered at their hands, the innovations in established custom and ritual and in the conventional governmental attributes of mercy, the "unwritten laws." So, when the Prometheus-Zeus conflict is represented also as the rebel versus tyrant conflict, it has been invested with a new probability. And men everywhere have felt, some obscurely and some clearly, an opposition between the animal and the spirit in man, between violence and persuasion, between might and intellect. So when the Zeus-Lygdamis versus Prometheus-rebel struggle is represented as another facet of the conflict between the two most powerful factors in human life—brute force and mind—the story has been invested with a new probability drawn from the community of man's experience. And men everywhere have known the torture of subjugation to a stronger force than themselves, have known the helplessness of persuasion against force, and yet have believed in the ultimate triumph of persuasion. And so, when the suffering Prometheus cries out in his helplessness and his knowledge, and doubts yet feels certain of the final outcome, the story has been invested with a new probability drawn from the community of man's experience. The original story of Zeus and Prometheus is like a stone thrown into a quiet pool, where the ripples spread in wider and wider circles.

Methods like the Aeschylean, developed to varying degrees of complexity, are familiar in other forms of literature. The degree of complexity is determined by the number of levels of meaning involved. For instance, in the *Pilgrim's Progress*, there is only one meaning in the tale apart from the highly dramatic story of Christian's journey, and that is the progress of the Christian soul toward the Eternal City. But, in the *Prometheus*, Aeschylus has made his story significant on a number of different levels, though each level involves the conflict of two opposing principles. For Prometheus is, politically, the symbol of the rebel against the tyrant who has overthrown the traditional rule of Justice and Law. He is the symbol of Knowledge against Force. He is symbolically the champion of man, raising him through the gift of intelligence, against the would-be destroyer of man. Finally, there is a level at which Prometheus is symbolically Man as opposed to God.

If we look at each of these patterns singly, we can see it progressively clarified in the characters and the plot, interlacing with one another, until the dramatist, having indicated all the issues between the two opposites, presumably found some compromise at which they were reconciled. Naturally, all the characters are not significant at all levels of the symbolism. That would be to demand of an artistic work the precision of a geometrical figure. But the central figure of Prometheus is significant at all levels, and on all levels the plot represents the strife between two opposing principles.

CHARACTER SYMBOLISM ON THE POLITICAL LEVEL

First, the pattern of Prometheus the rebel against the tyrant. Hephaestus' relation toward Zeus in the first scene is a very pregnant piece of political allegory. He is selected to be the instrument of the tyrant's vengeance because it is Hephaestus' privilege which Prometheus has given to man. Consequently, it is he who should most poignantly feel indignation at the theft. This is indeed called to his attention by Might (p. 37). But Hephaestus is unwilling to nail Prometheus down. His feeling of kinship is strong with him, stronger than any sense of right and wrong in this particular issue (p. 38), and he bitterly regrets that it should be his smithwork that will be responsible for Prometheus' tortures. Thus he represents the craftsman whose craft is used by the tyrant to serve the very ends to which he himself would least willingly see them applied. Over against Hephaestus—the artist who is tortured to do the will of the tyrant and suffers in doing it—are the two brutal instruments called Might and Violence, embodied qualities, creatures who have no life other than as functioning cogs in the tyrant's machine. The natural feeling of affinity of god with god (which matches the natural affinity of one man with another within the closely knit Greek community) must give place to the brutal demand of the tyrant.

Prometheus himself is the symbol of the clever man who lent assistance to the rising tyrant, only to find that by so doing he sowed the seeds of the distrust which is inherent in the unlawful seizure of political power and that on the first specific point of difference (in this case, disagreement about the future of man) gratitude for his political assistance not only is forgotten, but he himself is severely punished.[2] And it is as a political symbol that we must view Oceanus. He is the god who proved false to his kindred to placate the new tyrant. Now he believes that his influence with the enthroned sovereign is as great as his previous failure to oppose was important (see p. 49). Above all, in his conference

[2] See pp. 44–45.

with Prometheus he typifies the eternally compromising nature which is prepared to yield at every point in the certainty that resistance is in vain. The arguments adduced by Prometheus to bring about the abandonment of his mission as intermediary between Zeus and Prometheus are those designed to appeal to his placid cowardice. There is the fate of his kindred, for instance—the Giants whose attempts against Zeus he had failed to share—and the allusions to Typho's sufferings (p. 50). His daughters, the Oceanids, who constitute the Chorus of the play, are also political and human symbols. They represent the union of Oceanus' timid ignorance with an unswerving loyalty quite foreign to their father's nature. For with all their father's moderation—witness their repeated attempts to dissuade Prometheus from his attitude of intransigence—they still will not allow even their imminent destruction to interfere with their loyalty to their friend. "Tell us not to practice baseness," they say to Hermes in the last scene, when the thunder of Zeus is menacing them for their strong stand (p. 76). The Oceanids are the complement of their father. Right up to the end of the play the Chorus never believes in Prometheus' prophecy of the fall of Zeus. Oceanus never hears of it. But ignorance does not always mean lack of courage. Though both Oceanus and the Chorus of Oceanids typify the conventional as opposed to the extraordinary level of the hero's intelligence, the diversification of the choric standard is illuminating. The Oceanids do not understand, but they love their friend and will not leave him. Their father does not understand, but, without the anchor of their devotion, he drifts through vacillation and compromise to the abandonment of Prometheus.

CHARACTER SYMBOLISM ON THE LEVEL OF KNOWLEDGE VERSUS FORCE

Since Prometheus is the symbol of knowledge in its struggle against brute force, he is bound by the two servants of Zeus—Might and Violence. Knowledge is on his side, for in his conversation with the Chorus on page 45 we learn that he is the son of Earth, or Themis, and that she has told him the design of the future which is unshakable. Themis had told him in the old days of the struggle between Zeus and Kronos, that violence would never win the day (p. 45), and he had endeavored in vain to convince his brother-Titans that they must work by strategy rather than by force if they were to conquer. It is in virtue of this knowledge that he possesses a sure confidence that Zeus will ultimately be vanquished. The secret itself, the knowledge of which enables Prometheus to be brave in the face of torture, is a symbol of the ultimate superiority of knowledge over force. Aeschylus is at great pains to define exactly what he means by the immutable design of fate (of which Prometheus has the secret) as opposed to any power which Zeus may temporarily possess over Prometheus or over the world. In the dialogue between Prometheus and the Chorus on page 55, the Chorus says:

Therefore do not help mortals beyond all expediency while neglecting yourself in your troubles. For I am of good hope that once freed of these bonds you will be no less in power than Zeus.

PROMETHEUS: Not yet has fate that brings to fulfilment determined these things to be thus. I must be twisted by ten thousand pangs and agonies, as I now am, to escape my chains at last. Craft is far weaker than necessity.

CHORUS: Who then is the steersman of necessity?

PROMETHEUS: The triple formed Fates and the remembering Furies.

CHORUS: Is Zeus weaker than these?

PROMETHEUS: Yes, for he, too, cannot escape what is fated.

CHORUS: What is fated for Zeus besides eternal sovereignty?

PROMETHEUS: Inquire of this no further, do not entreat me.

CHORUS: This is some solemn secret, I suppose, that you are hiding.

PROMETHEUS: Think of some other story: this one it is not yet the season to give tongue to, but it must be hidden with all care; for it is only by keeping it that I will escape my despiteful bondage and my agony.[3]

[3] There is no explicit statement throughout the play that destiny is always just, even in the long run. That conclusion is clearly implied, however, in the way in which Prometheus appeals to the powers to

This knowledge, in its alliance with the higher power of destiny, is contrasted forcibly with both the ignorance of the servants of the tyrant, Might and Violence, and the ignorance of Zeus himself. For instance, Might says on page 39:

There is nothing without discomfort involved except the overlordship of the Gods. For only Zeus is free.

And again on page 41:

The Gods named you wrongly when they called you Forethought; you yourself *need* Forethought, ... , etc.

The ignorance of Zeus is manifested in his dispatch of the god Hermes to compel Prometheus, under threat of further torture, to reveal the secret which shall ultimately unseat Zeus from heaven.

PROMETHEUS AS THE CHAMPION OF MAN AGAINST THE PERSECUTOR OF MAN

On the third level of character symbolism Prometheus is the champion of man against Zeus, the persecutor of man. First, after his success in heaven, Zeus was fain to destroy man and make another creature in his place. We are not

---

witness his unjust treatment (p. 41, 77); and it is explicitly stated constantly throughout the Agamemnon trilogy, where the same distinction is made between the power of Zeus and the power of Fate (cf. *Choephoroi* 61–65; *Eumenides* 1045–46). Finally, in the *Oresteia*, the will of Zeus would be synonymous with *Moira*. This end has not yet been attained in the *Prometheus vinctus*. It is obvious that Aeschylus conceives of much personal injustice as part of the scheme of fate for the world in general. We do not need to look further than the example of Io, whose torture at the hands of Zeus and wanderings through the world are all part of the design of fate which will bring her to the land of Nile and the birth of Epaphos. Prometheus himself is a sufferer in order that the will of fate may be fulfilled. In the passage quoted above, he tells how his "ten thousand tortures and pangs" are part of fate's plan, and on p. 47 he says: "I knew when I transgressed nor will deny it. In helping man I brought my troubles on me." It appears, then, that Aeschylus conceives of a generally just principle immanent in the working of the world, the manifestation of which, however, in the case of any single individual unit, from the short-range point of view of the individual, may be unjust.

told explicitly why Zeus wished to destroy man. There is no
indication what sort of animal he wished to put in his place;
but, in so far as Prometheus in disobedience to Zeus en-
lightened man by the gift of intelligence, it may be assumed
that Zeus's creation would have had no such dangerous po-
tentialities of development. This first attempt to destroy
mankind is almost certainly the flood of Deucalion, of which
we hear elsewhere, and there is a tradition to the effect that
Prometheus counseled Deucalion to the building of the ark
which preserved him and his family. The second action in
Prometheus' rescue of man from the enmity of the world in
which he found himself is even more significant. "I stopped
mortals from foreseeing doom," says Prometheus (p. 46).

CHORUS: What cure did you provide them with against that
sickness?
PROMETHEUS: I placed in them blind hopes.
CHORUS: That was a great gift you gave to men.

As the rest of his gifts to man are all concerned with enlightenment,[4] and, indeed, fire itself becomes a symbol of
that enlightenment, this gift of "blind hopes" seems at first
strange. Yet it is quite consistent. There is a passage in the
Gorgias which is illuminating here.[5] We are told that in the
days of Kronos and *when Zeus was newly king*, men were in-
formed as to the day of their death and were judged alive
with all their clothes on and their possessions about them by
live judges. This was a practice which brought much injustice, says Plato, and Zeus ultimately ordered it otherwise.
Now Plato is using the myth for the illustration of his own
theme, and we must not be surprised that his picture of the
development of man when this was the state of things does
not accord with that of Aeschylus. But the dating in the case
of Plato shows either that he and Aeschylus were drawing on
the same myth or else that Plato is borrowing from Aeschy-

[4] See: "I found them witless and gave them the use of their wits
and made them masters of their minds," and the entire passage de-
scribing the evolution of man under the guidance of Prometheus
(pp. 53–54). All the arts of life and the practical devices of reason
against environment were suggested by Prometheus.

[5] *Gorgias* 523 A.

lus: "In the days of Kronos and when Zeus was still newly king." What, then, is the meaning of the blind hopes which were the compensation for man's loss of knowledge of his death and yet left him able to use his reason to build houses and yoke horses and invent cures for sickness?

Let us recur to the nature of Prometheus' knowledge. He is wise in the wisdom of his mother Themis, or Earth, and consequently wise in the knowledge of destiny. This is not reason. It is knowledge absolute. The knowledge of the day of a man's death partakes of that quality, for it is in the province of destiny. So man at the beginning had an infinitely small particle of the *same kind of knowledge* which Prometheus enjoyed in large measure. Just as animals today seem to have a curious intuition of the coming of their death and crawl away into hiding to face it, so primitive man had this knowledge. And Prometheus caused them to cease to foreknow the day of their death. For the gift of reason, the supreme ally in their struggle against nature, made them fight on against death in "blind hope," even when the day of their death had come. It is worth noticing here that, of the two accounts of man's origins in the world—the one that of a golden age of material and moral perfection[6] and the other of miserable ignorance and helplessness—Aeschylus has preferred the scientific tradition. But he has chosen to incorporate in his account a grain of the truth of the former. The very small particle of absolute knowledge which man possessed was a spark of the divine. The fire itself, Prometheus' greatest and most celebrated gift to man, is a symbol of practical, not speculative, reason. And nowhere does Aeschylus assert that such speculative reason in its fulness will ever be in man's possession.

PROMETHEUS AS THE SYMBOL OF MAN

The last level of symbolism shows Prometheus not merely as the champion of man but in some way as the symbol of man himself in his conflict against powers which control him in his helplessness. It is the story of the man-god who must

[6] Hesiod *Works and Days* 109.

suffer for his kindness to man by having his state equated with theirs. In the case of Prometheus the good which is achieved for man is achieved before the suffering (which comes in the nature of a punishment). In the case of Christ the punishment is in a mystical sense the direct antecedent of the benefit which man will obtain. The cry of Prometheus on page 47—

> I knew when I transgressed nor will deny it.
> In helping man I brought my troubles on me;
> but yet I did not think that with such tortures
> I should be wasted on these airy cliffs—

is the cry of the Savior who is man enough to be weak under pain. Without this sense of kinship with man, no tragic hero can communicate his tragedy. It is the Christ on the cross who cries, "God, why hast thou forsaken me?" The essence of this symbolism is that Prometheus, though possessed of a knowledge of destiny and therefore of victory in the end, should for the present be at the mercy of a brutal and ignorant opponent. So, too, is the mortal Io. So are all the mortals over whom Death holds power against which they fight with "blind hopes." Finally, on this symbolic level there is Prometheus' deliverance by Heracles, who is part god and part man. This once again binds his fate to the creature whom he has helped to survive in the teeth of the opposition of the supreme god.[7]

[7] We should notice that there are two parts to Prometheus' rescue from his present suffering. The one is his actual deliverance by Heracles (p. 65); the other is his reconciliation with Zeus elicited by the threat of the secret. On p. 47 Prometheus announces that a term will be placed to his pain only "when Zeus decides." This is in line with the general prediction of Themis that "not by force but by craft shall the conquerors win the victory." It would be inconsistent with the opposition between Prometheus as Wisdom and Zeus as Violence if Prometheus were to win by means of his adversary's weapons. Yet in view of p. 65 it is plain that Heracles delivers him and that the reconciliation with Zeus is the reinstatement of Prometheus in his former honors in heaven. This must be the meaning of the "recompense" (p. 43) which Zeus will be forced to pay the Titan. We may wonder whether the release of Prometheus from his rock was effected with the consent of Zeus or without it. For on p. 65 Io asks, "Who will release you

So much for the symbols superimposed one on another in the structure of the play. There still remains to be seen what is the nature of the dramatic process in this symbolic form of drama. What I have attempted so far is to show that the character of Prometheus does not have a single particular aspect but rather a number of aspects on various levels, each level being worked out into an integrated whole, and that the story of Prometheus on these several levels is the symbol of all manner of movements in heaven and earth from the rebel against the tyrant to man against god.

PLOT

As I have indicated before, narrative takes the place of action, and the play may be divided into acts according to the interlocutor of Prometheus involved. The first act is the nailing of Prometheus by Might and Violence aided by Hephaestus; the second, the dialogue between Prometheus and the Chorus; the third, between Prometheus and Oceanus; the fourth, between Prometheus and the Chorus; the fifth, between Prometheus and Io; the sixth, a short one, with the Chorus again; and, finally, the Epilogue, like the Prologue, brings Prometheus openly face to face with his enemies, who again use the only weapon they have against him—cruelty and violence. The progressive clarification of the issues between the two opposites on all the levels is conditioned by the character of Prometheus' interlocutors. The Chorus holds a dual position in this play of gods and demigods: it is part the conventional listener and norm of conduct, part also a close friend of Prometheus. It finally manifests its loyalty and affection for him in the most unusual and

---

against the will of Zeus?" and the answer, "It is Fate's will that one of your [Io's] descendants shall be the deliverer," assumes that he will do so "against the will of Zeus." But there were apparently compromises on the side of Prometheus; for Hermes on p. 75 at least threatens that some god must be found who is willing to be a substitute for Prometheus and surrender his immortality, and the legend recounts that such a sacrifice was made by the centaur Chiron, already in deathly agony as the result of Heracles' arrow, yet condemned by his godhead to an immortality of pain.

striking way by consenting to suffer along with him. To the Chorus, Prometheus' personal troubles of the past are unfolded, both as concerns man and as concerns the general political issue. Oceanus is significant only on the political issue, and so in the scenes with him nothing about man or the ultimate hope of deliverance based on the knowledge of Destiny is explained. For Io, both as a fellow-sufferer at the hands of the tyrant Zeus and as the future mother of Prometheus' deliverer who shall be the demigod, the exposition of the three themes—that of man, that of wisdom, and the political issue—are pertinent. The fourth theme, the man-god against Zeus, is explained in Prometheus' own person alone, in the thought of the entire piece, and in the violence of the Prologue and the Epilogue. In the long stretches of narration, each one probing the further recesses of the particular level of symbols at which it works, we have the ancient counterpart of Mr. Bloom's interior monologue.

The statement of the drama is an exposition of the present entirely in terms of the past and the future.[8] The present, as present, is relevant only in so far as it illustrates Prometheus' helplessness in the face of Zeus's power. It is, as I have remarked before, the level of the suffering Prometheus-Christ; but this level can be made articulate only by the comment of the spectators, as in the initial expressions of grief on the part of the Chorus, or by the occasional outbursts of Prometheus himself or by the opening and closing scenes of physical suffering.

In the first scene, to the accompaniment of the blows dealt by the unwilling Hephaestus, we have the past and the future expressed in their simplest terms. The past is the sin of Prometheus in giving fire to man; the future is, in the opinion of Might, endless suffering for Prometheus until he learns, "for all his wit, that he is duller than Zeus" (p. 39).[9]

[8] This division for the first scene is worked out in George Thomson's edition of the *Prometheus Bound* (Cambridge: Cambridge University Press, 1932).

[9] There is, of course, dramatic irony in the words of Might, "From which of your sufferings will your mortals be able to relieve you?" since the audience is aware that the deliverer is to be Heracles, half-man, half-god.

When the torturers are gone, Prometheus' soliloquy on page 41 gives the simplest statement of the past, present, and future scheme again, but with the additional fact established that Prometheus' vision is superior to that of Might in virtue of Prometheus' parentage. This enables him to know that the result of the torture will not be what Might imagines (see p. 37) nor will it be eternal, as is insinuated on page 41. Hence, we have our knowledge versus brute force dialectic with its first postulate: the superior nature of Prometheus' knowledge.

In Prometheus' dialogue with the Chorus on pages 43–44 we have a further clarification of the future. We learn now, not only that Prometheus knows a conclusion different from that adumbrated in the first scene, but that it is a secret in Prometheus' possession which shall unseat the tyrant and that only contrition and reparation on the part of Zeus will induce Prometheus to disclose this secret. So up to the present we have the theme of the champion of man against his persecutor and the contest between knowledge and brute force. On page 44 we revert to the past, and we now see the beginnings of the political myth. Also a clear distinction is made between the two symbolic levels— Prometheus the benefactor of man and Prometheus the rebel against the tyrant Zeus (pp. 45–46). They are tied together by the cunning statement that the predisposing cause for Zeus's distrust of Prometheus was the uneasy sense of benefits received, and the championship of man was the specific *aitia* of which he availed himself to condemn his erstwhile supporter. On the political level Prometheus takes his account into the past when Zeus-Peisistratus (or Cypselus or Lygdamis) was seeking support for his attempt upon the legitimate monarch, his own father Kronos. This part he sums up in the words, "It is the disease of tyranny not to trust its friends" (p. 45). We then pass on straight to Prometheus' help to man. The past is now beginning to be clearer. We can see that Zeus's conduct, which up to now has been explained purely as a punishment inflicted on an offense of a god against a god (p. 41), has deeper roots. It is fixed not only in Prometheus' help to man but also in the past of Zeus himself. In the account of the championship of man we hear first of the rescue from the flood,[10] but that is followed by the statement of Prometheus' gift of intelligence to man, most concretely instanced by the granting of fire.

The entrance of Oceanus brings us back to the strictly political myth in the past. Oceanus is the timorous adherent of the tyrant, whose indifference may have some value to Zeus-Peisistratus on his upward path but whose value is now negligible. No editor, as far as I know, until the publication of the recent excellent translation of Miss Edith Hamilton,[11] has realized the irony of Prometheus' treatment of this figure. This ancient god enters riding on a hippocampus, and we have allusions to this rather comic monster. There is nothing but mocking laughter in Prometheus' first remarks, and there is contemptuous scorn in "I envy you, since you have kept out of the range of accusation, you who bore hand and daring with me in all." There is no record in the rest of the play or in mythology, as far as I can discover, of any assistance ever lent to rebels by the chicken-hearted Oceanus. The words of Prometheus are, I suggest, pure sarcasm like his greeting:

Have you, too, come to gape in wonder at this great display, my torture [p. 48]?

For Oceanus' pacific mission as intermediary he has only the caustic comment that he sees in it "nothing but unnecessary trouble and empty-headed, silly good nature." Prometheus knows that Oceanus is an insignificant light-weight; and it is clear that Aeschylus is using the scene to show the part played by the silly, cowardly, and yet not ill-natured partisans of the tyrant. Besides, for Prometheus there can be no compromise on terms of apology and explanation. There must be a logical conclusion to the essentially intellectual and moral differences between himself and Zeus.

The complete exposition of Oceanus' point of view makes

[10] This is presumably the meaning on p. 45: "I rescued men, etc."
[11] *Three Greek Plays* (New York: W. W. Norton Co., 1937).

it unnecessary for Prometheus to embroider at greater length the aspects of the political squabble with Zeus before man became a factor in the quarrel (p. 53). But the rejection of Oceanus' advice, an advice which the Chorus itself is more than half-disposed to approve, forces Prometheus to tell of his aims in the succor of mankind in order to avoid the charge of obstinacy (p. 53). Thus the transition from one level to the other is made very naturally, following a natural trend of thought in the previous scene. So we get the final clarification of the championship of man in the past in its most significant form (p. 54).

On page 55 we have a further explanation of the future on the level of knowledge versus brute force. It is the clear statement of the circumstances which make it impossible that Zeus's rule over the world can be eternal. It is a corollary of the statement of the nature of Prometheus' knowledge. On page 45 we learned that Necessity is unconquerable and that Prometheus' mother is acquainted with the designs of destiny. Now we are told the exact nature of the relation of Zeus's power to the inexorable destiny. We do not yet know, however, in what way destiny will interfere in Zeus's plans for eternal lordship.

The episode of Io which follows is at first sight the most puzzling thing in the play. It is very long and looks like a poetic geographical tour of the Greek world. However, a closer study will show Io's integral relation to the play as a whole. She is, as I have said before, the one of the three friendly interlocutors to whom the culmination of everything on three levels—wisdom versus force, champion of man versus persecutor of man, rebel versus tyrant—in the future can be explained. So we have the final story of the secret which will cause Zeus's fall (pp. 64–65), the explanation of the marriage and the part played by it in forcing from Zeus an acknowledgment of the injustice done to Prometheus. We have the culmination of the championship of man theme; for Heracles, who will deliver Prometheus, is that culmination, being half-man, half-god, and the highest evolution of the animal to whom Prometheus granted intelligence as the first step up from the primeval slime. And on page 70 the threat to the tyrant, the loss of the throne, is the last step but one in the revelation of the movement started when Prometheus backed Zeus in his revolt against his father. Even the long arid stretches of geography have a contrapuntal value in the structure of the trilogy, for from the fragments it is apparent that they match the wanderings of Heracles in the second play. Possibly also George Thomson is right in conjecturing that both Io and Heracles are parts of a further symbolism, Io the moon and Heracles the zodiac, and possibly the thirty thousand years of Prometheus' imprisonment signify the cycle of time in the Orphic tradition.[12]

Again it is worth noticing how appositely the entrance of Io is prepared by the choral ode which asks, "What help can there be for you in creatures of a day?" (p. 56). She, as the future ancestor of Heracles, is to furnish the answer to the question. The Chorus on page 69 with their speculations on the unwisdom of such unequal marriages as those of Io lead the thought naturally to the last of the dialogues between themselves and Prometheus. The future of Zeus's marriage, the birth of the son who shall overthrow the father, is now the most engrossing theme for Prometheus. In this dialogue and in the last scene with Hermes he no longer speaks as if the secret were to be a means of bargaining. It is now the hope cherished by Prometheus that he will one day see his hated enemy plunged into such misery as his own. He must know, as the decrees of destiny are absolute, that no such punishment will be accorded him as satisfaction, that Zeus will necessarily make terms. But at the moment of his blind rage he chooses to picture rather the hurt of a foe than the benefit to himself. It is a subtle psychological touch for the ending of the first part of the trilogy.

[12] Thomson, *op. cit.*, p. 38.

PROMETHEUS BOUND

SCENE: *A bare and desolate crag in the Caucasus. Enter Might and Violence, demons, servants of Zeus, and Hephaestus, the Smith. The demons are represented by abstract masks, with nothing personal or individual in their expression.*

* * *

MIGHT

This is the world's limit that we have come to; this is the Scythian country, an untrodden desolation. Hephaestus, it is you that must heed the commands the Father laid upon you to nail this malefactor to the high craggy rocks in fetters unbreakable of adamantine chain. For it was your flower, the brightness of fire that devises all, that he stole and gave to mortal men; this is the sin for which he must pay the Gods the penalty—that he may learn to endure and like the sovereignty of Zeus and quit his man-loving disposition.

HEPHAESTUS

Might and Violence, in you the command of Zeus has its perfect fulfilment: in you there is nothing to stand in its way. But, for myself, I have not the heart to bind violently a God who is my kin here on this wintry cliff. Yet there is constraint upon me to have the heart for just that, for it is a dangerous thing to treat the Father's words lightly.

High-contriving Son of Themis of Straight Counsel: this is not of your will nor of mine, yet I shall nail you in bonds of indissoluble bronze on this crag far from men. Here you shall hear no voice of mortal; here you shall see no form of mortal. You shall be grilled by the sun's bright fire and change the fair bloom of your skin. You shall be glad when Night comes with her mantle of stars and hides the sun's light; but the sun shall scatter the hoar-frost again at dawn. Always the grievous burden of your torture will be there to

37

wear you down; for he that shall cause it to cease has yet to be born.

Such is the reward you reap of your man-loving disposition. For you, a God, feared not the anger of the Gods, but gave honors to mortals beyond what was just. Wherefore you shall mount guard on this unlovely rock, upright, sleepless, not bending the knee. Many a groan and many a lamentation you shall utter, but they shall not serve you. For the mind of Zeus is hard to soften with prayer, and every ruler is harsh whose rule is new.

MIGHT

Come, why are you holding back? Why are you spending a useless pity? Why is it that you do not hate a God whom the Gods hate most of all? Why do you not hate him, since it was your honor that he betrayed to men?

HEPHAESTUS

Our kinship has strange power; that, and our life together.

MIGHT

Yes. But to turn a deaf ear to the Father's words—how can that be? Do you not fear that more?

HEPHAESTUS

You are always pitiless, always full of ruthlessness.

MIGHT

There is no good singing dirges over him. It is you who spend your labor uselessly at a task that doesn't help.

HEPHAESTUS

O handicraft of mine—that I deeply hate!

MIGHT

Why do you hate it? In simple frankness be it said, your craft is in no way the author of his present troubles.

HEPHAESTUS

Yet would another had had this craft allotted to him.

MIGHT

There is nothing without discomfort involved except the overlordship of the Gods. For only Zeus is free.

HEPHAESTUS

I know. I have no answer to this.

MIGHT

Hurry now. Throw the chain around him that the Father may not look upon your tarrying.

HEPHAESTUS

There are the fetters, there: you can see them.

MIGHT

Put them on his hands: strong, now with the hammer: strike. Nail him to the rock.

HEPHAESTUS

It is being done now. I am not idling at my work.

MIGHT

Hammer it more; put in the wedge; leave it loose nowhere. He's a cunning fellow at finding a way even out of hopeless difficulties.

HEPHAESTUS

Look now, his arm is fixed immovably!

MIGHT

Nail the other safe, that he may learn, for all his cleverness, that he is duller-witted than Zeus.

HEPHAESTUS

No one, save Prometheus, can justly blame me.

MIGHT

Drive the obstinate jaw of the adamantine wedge right through his breast: drive it hard.

HEPHAESTUS

Alas, Prometheus, I groan for your sufferings.

MIGHT

Are you pitying again? Are you groaning for the enemies of Zeus? Have a care, lest some day you may be pitying yourself.

HEPHAESTUS

You see a sight that hurts the eye.

MIGHT

I see this rascal getting his deserts. Throw the girth around his sides.

HEPHAESTUS

I am forced to do this; do not keep urging me.

MIGHT

Yes, I will urge you, and hound you on as well. Get below now, and hoop his legs in strongly.

HEPHAESTUS

There now, the task is done. It has not taken long.

MIGHT

Hammer the piercing fetters with all your power, for the Overseer of our work is severe.

HEPHAESTUS

Your looks and the refrain of your tongue are alike.

MIGHT

You can be soft-hearted. But do not blame my stubbornness and harshness of temper.

HEPHAESTUS

Let us go. He has the harness on his limbs.

MIGHT (*to Prometheus*)

Now, play the insolent: now, plunder the Gods' privileges
and give them to creatures of a day. What drop of your
sufferings can mortals spare you? The Gods named you
wrongly when they called you Forethought; you yourself
need Forethought to extricate yourself from this contrivance.

(*Prometheus is left alone on the rock.*)

PROMETHEUS

Bright light, swift-winged winds, springs of the rivers, num-
berless laughter of the sea's waves, earth, mother of all, and
the all-seeing circle of the sun: I call upon you to see what I,
a God, suffer at the hands of Gods,—
See with what kind of torture
worn down I shall wrestle ten thousand
years of time—
such is the bond of despite that the Prince
has devised against me, the new Prince
of the Blessed Ones. O woe is me!
I groan for the present sorrow,
I groan for the sorrow to come, I groan
questioning when there shall come a time
when He shall ordain a limit to my sufferings.
What am I saying? I have known all before,
all that shall be, and clearly known; to me
nothing that hurts shall come with a new face.
So must I bear, as lightly as I can
the destiny that fate has given me;
for I know well against necessity,
against its strength no one can fight and win.

I cannot speak about my fortune, cannot
hold my tongue either. It was mortal man
to whom I gave great privileges and
for that was yoked in this unyielding harness.
I hunted out the secret spring of fire,
that filled the narthex stem, which when revealed
became the teacher of each craft to men,

a great resource. This is the sin committed
for which I stand accountant and I pay
nailed in my chains under the open sky.

What is that? the rustle
of birds' wings near? the air whispers
with the gentle strokes of wings.
Everything that comes toward me is occasion for fear.

CHORUS

Fear not: this is a company of friends
that comes to your mountain with swift
rivalry of wings.
Hardly have we persuaded our father's
mind: and the quick bearing winds
speeded us hither. The sound
of stroke of bronze rang through our cavern
in its depths and it shook from us
shamefaced modesty; unsandalled
we have hastened on our chariot of wings.

PROMETHEUS

Alas children of teeming Tethys and of him
who encircles all the world with stream unsleeping,
Father Ocean,
look, see with what chains
I am nailed on the craggy heights
of this gully to keep a watch
that none would envy me.

CHORUS

I see, Prometheus: and a mist of fear and tears
besets my eyes as I see your form
wasting away on these cliffs
in adamantine bonds of bitter shame.
For new are the steersmen that rule Olympus:
and new are the customs by which Zeus rules,
customs that have no law to them,
but what was great before he brings to nothingness.

PROMETHEUS

Would that he had hurled me
underneath the earth and underneath
the house of Hades, host to the dead—
yes, down to limitless Tartarus,
yes, though he bound me cruelly
in chains unbreakable,
so neither God nor any other being
might have found joy in gloating over me.
Now as I hang, the plaything of the winds,
my enemies can laugh at what I suffer.

CHORUS

Who of the Gods is so hard of heart
that he finds joy in this?
Who is there that does not feel
sorrow answering your pain?
save only Zeus; for he malignantly
always cherishing a mind
that bends not has subdued the breed
of Uranos nor shall he cease
until he satisfies his heart,
or someone take the rule from him—that hard-to-capture
    rule—
by some device of subtlety.

PROMETHEUS

Yes, there shall come a day for me
when he shall need me, me that now am tortured
in bonds and fetters—he shall need me then—
this president of the Blessed—
to show the new plot whereby he may be spoiled
of his throne and his power.
Then not with honeyed tongues
of persuasion shall he enchant me:
he shall not cow me with his threats
to tell him what I know,
until he free me from my cruel chains
and pay me recompense for what I suffer.

Chorus

You are stout of heart, unyielding
to the bitterness of pain.
You are free of tongue, too free.
It is my mind that piercing fear has fluttered,
your misfortunes frighten me.
Where and when is it fated
to see you reach the term, to see you reach
the harbour free of trouble at the last?
A disposition none can win, a heart
that no persuasions soften—these are his,
the Son of Kronos.

Prometheus

I know that he is savage: and his justice
a thing he keeps by his own standard: still
that will of his shall melt to softness yet
when he is broken in the way I know,
and though his temper now is oaken hard
it shall be softened: hastily he'll come
to meet my haste, to join in amity
and union with me—one day he shall come.

Chorus

Reveal it all to us: tell us the story of what the charge was
on which Zeus caught you and punished you so cruelly with
such dishonour. Tell us, if the telling will not injure you in
any way.

Prometheus

To speak of this is bitterness. To keep silent
bitter no less; and every way is misery.

When first the Gods began their angry quarrel,
and God matched God in rising faction,—some
eager to drive old Kronos from his throne
that Zeus might rule—the fools!—others again
earnest, that Zeus might never be their king—
I then with the best counsel tried to win

the Titans, sons of Uranos and Earth,
but failed. They would have none of crafty schemes
and in their savage arrogance of spirit
thought they would lord it easily by force.
But she that was my mother, Themis, Earth,—
she is but one although her names are many—
had prophesied to me how it should be,
even how the fates decreed it: and she said
"that not by strength nor overmastering force
the fates allowed the conquerors to conquer
but by guile only": this is what I told them,
but they would not vouchsafe a glance at me.
Then with those things before me it seemed best
to take my mother and join Zeus' side:
he was as willing as we were:
thanks to my plans the dark receptacle
of Tartarus conceals the ancient Kronos,
him and his allies. These were the services
I rendered to this tyrant and these pains
the payment he has given me in requital.
This is a sickness rooted and inherent
in the nature of a tyranny:
that he that holds it does not trust his friends.

But you have asked on what particular
charge he now tortures me: this I will tell you.
As soon as he ascended to the throne,
that was his father's, straightway he assigned
to the several Gods their several privileges
and portioned out the power, but to the unhappy
breed of mankind he gave no heed, intending
to blot the race out and create a new.
Against these plans none stood save I: I dared.
l rescued men from shattering destruction
that would have carried them to Hades' house;
and therefore I am tortured on this rock,
a bitterness to suffer, and a pain
to pitiful eyes. I gave to mortal man
a precedence over myself in pity: I

can win no pity: pitiless is he
that thus chastises me, a spectacle
bringing dishonor on the name of Zeus.

CHORUS
He would be ironminded and made of stone, indeed, Prometheus, who did not sympathize with your sufferings. I would not have chosen to see them and now that I see my heart is pained.

PROMETHEUS
Yes, to my friends I am pitiable to see.

CHORUS
Did you perhaps go further than you have told us?

PROMETHEUS
I caused mortals to cease foreseeing doom.

CHORUS
What cure did you provide them with against that sickness?

PROMETHEUS
I placed in them blind hopes.

CHORUS
That was a great gift you gave to men.

PROMETHEUS
Besides this, I gave them fire.

CHORUS
And do creatures of a day now possess bright faced fire?

PROMETHEUS
Yes, and from it they shall learn many crafts.

CHORUS
Then these are the charges on which—

PROMETHEUS
Zeus tortures me and gives me no respite.

CHORUS
Is there no limit set for your pain?

PROMETHEUS
None save when it shall seem good to Zeus.

CHORUS
How will it ever seem good to him? What hope is there?
Do you not see how you have erred? It is not pleasure for
me to say that you have erred, and for you it is a pain to
hear. But let us speak no more of all this and do you seek
some means of deliverance from your trials.

PROMETHEUS
It is an easy thing for one whose foot
is on the outside of calamity
to give advice and to rebuke the sufferer.
I have known all that you have said: I knew,
I knew when I transgressed nor will deny it.
In helping man I brought my troubles on me;
but yet I did not think that with such tortures
I should be wasted on these airy cliffs,
this lonely mountain top, with no one near.
But do not sorrow for my present suffering;
alight on earth and hear what is to come
that you may know the whole complete: I beg you,
alight; and join your sorrow with mine: misfortune
wandering the same track lights now upon one
and now upon another.

CHORUS
                    willing our ears,
that hear you cry to them, Prometheus,
now with light foot I leave the rushing car
and sky, the holy path of birds, and light
upon this jutting rock: I long
to hear your story to the end.

(Enter Oceanos, riding on a hippocamp, or sea monster.)

OCEANOS

                    I come
on a long journey, speeding past the boundaries,
to visit you, Prometheus: with the mind
alone, no bridle needed, I direct
my heavy-winged bird; my heart is sore
for your misfortunes; you know that. I think,
that it is kinship makes me feel them so.
Besides, apart from kinship, there is no one
I hold in higher estimation: that
you soon shall know and know beside that in me
there is no mere word-kindness: tell me
how I can help you, and you will never say
that you have any friend more loyal to you
than Oceanos.

PROMETHEUS

What do I see? Have you, too, come to gape
in wonder at this great display, my torture?
How did you have the courage to come here
to this land, Iron-Mother, leaving the stream
called after you and the rock-roofed selfestablished
caverns? was it to feast your eyes upon
the spectacle of my suffering and join
in pity for my pain? Now look and see
the sight, this friend of Zeus, that helped set up
his tyranny and see what agonies
twist me, by his instructions!

OCEANOS

                  Yes, I see,
Prometheus, and I want, indeed I do,
to advise you for the best, for all your cleverness.
Know yourself and reform your ways to new ways,
for new he is that rules among the Gods.
But if you throw about such angry words,
words that are whetted swords, soon Zeus will hear you,
even though his seat in glory is far removed,

and then your present multitude of pains
will seem like childsplay. My poor friend, give up
this angry mood of yours and look for means
of getting yourself free of trouble. Maybe
what I say seems to you both old and commonplace;
but this is what you pay, Prometheus, for
that tongue of yours which talked so high and haughty:
you are not yet humble, still you do not yield
to your misfortunes, and you wish, indeed,
to add some more to them; now if you follow
me as a schoolmaster you will not kick
against the pricks, seeing that he, the King,
that rules alone, is harsh and sends accounts
to no one's audit for the deeds he does.
Now I will go and try if I can free you:
do you be quiet, do not talk so much.
Since your mind is so subtle, don't you know
that a vain tongue is subject to correction?

PROMETHEUS

I envy you, that you stand clear of blame,
yet shared and dared in everything with me!
Now let me be, and have no care for me.
Do what you will, Him you will not persuade;
He is not easily won over: look,
take care lest coming here to me should hurt you.

OCEANOS

You have been always better at advising
others than you yourself. I take my cue
from deeds, not words. Do not withhold me now
when I am eager to go to Zeus. I'm sure,
I'm sure that he will grant this favor to me,
to free you from your chains.

PROMETHEUS

I thank you and will never cease: for loyalty
is not what you are wanting in. Don't trouble,

for you will trouble to no purpose, and no help
to me—if it so be you want to trouble.
No, rest yourself, keep away from this thing;
because I am unlucky I would not,
for that, have everyone unlucky too.
No: for my heart is sore already when
I think about my brothers' fortunes—Atlas
who stands to westwards of the world supporting
the pillar of earth and heaven on his shoulders,
a load that suits no shoulders; and the earthborn
dweller in caves Cilician, whom I saw
and pitied, hundred-headed, dreadful monster,
fierce Typho, conquered and brought low by force.
Once against all the Gods he stood, opposing,
hissing out terror from his grim jaws; his eyes
flashed gorgon glaring lightning as he thought
to sack the sovereign tyranny of Zeus,
but upon him came the unsleeping bolt
of Zeus, the lightning breathing flame, down rushing,
which cast him from his high aspiring boast,
struck to the heart, his strength was blasted dead
and burnt to ashes; now a sprawling mass
useless he lies, hard by the narrow seaway
pressed down beneath the roots of Aetna: high
above him on the mountain peak the smith
Hephaestus works at the anvil. Yet one day
there shall burst out rivers of fire, devouring,
with savage jaws the fertile level plains
of Sicily of the fair fruits; such boiling wrath
with weapons of fire-breathing surf, a fiery
unapproachable torrent, shall Typho vomit,
though Zeus' lightning left him but a cinder.

But all of this you know: you do not need me
to be your schoolmaster: reassure yourself
as you know how: this cup I shall drain myself
till the high mind of Zeus shall cease from anger.

OCEANOS

Do you not know, Prometheus, that words are healers of the sick temper?

PROMETHEUS

Yes, if in season due one soothes the heart with them, not tries violently to reduce the swelling anger.

OCEANOS

Tell me, what danger do you see for me in loyalty to you, and courage therein?

PROMETHEUS

I see only useless effort and a silly good nature.

OCEANOS

Suffer me then to be sick of this sickness for it is a profitable thing, if one is wise, to seem foolish.

PROMETHEUS

This shall seem to be my fault.

OCEANOS

Clearly your words send me home again.

PROMETHEUS

Yes, lest your doings for me bring you enmity.

OCEANOS

His enmity, who newly sits on the all-powerful throne?

PROMETHEUS

His is a heart you should beware of vexing.

OCEANOS

Your own misfortune will be my teacher, Prometheus.

PROMETHEUS

Off with you, then! Begone! Keep your present mind.

OCEANOS

These words fall on very responsive ears. Already my four-
legged bird is pawing the level track of Heaven with his
wings and he will be glad to bend the knee in his own stable.

CHORUS

Strophe

I cry aloud, Prometheus, and lament your bitter fate,
my tender eyes are trickling tears:
their fountains wet my cheek.
This is a tyrant's deed, this is unlovely,
a thing done by a tyrant's private laws,
and with this thing Zeus shows his haughtiness
of temper towards the Gods that were of old.

Antistrophe

Now all the earth has cried aloud, lamenting:
now all that was magnificent of old
laments your fall, laments your brethren's fall
from honorable station. All those men,
as many as in holy Asia hold
their stablished habitation, all lament
in sympathy for your most grievous woes.

Strophe B

Dwellers in the land of Colchis,
maidens, fearless in the fight,
and the host of Scythia, living
round the lake Maeotis, living
on the edges of the world

Antistrophe B

And Arabia's flower of warriors
and the craggy fortress keepers
near Caucasian mountains, fighters
terrible, crying for battle,
brandishing sharp pointed spears.

Strophe

One God and one God only I have seen
before this day, in torture and in bonds

unbreakable: he was a Titan,
Atlas, whose strength and might
ever exceeded; now he bends his back
and groans beneath the load of earth and heaven.

Antistrophe

The wave cries out as it breaks into surf;
the depth cries out, lamenting you; the dark
Hades, the hollow underneath the world,
sullenly groans below; the springs
of sacred flowing rivers all lament
the pain and pity of your suffering.

PROMETHEUS

Do not think that out of pride or stubbornness I hold my peace; my heart is eaten away when I am aware of myself, when I see myself insulted as I am. Who was it but I who in truth dispensed their honors to these new gods? I will say nothing of this; you know it all; but hear what troubles there were among men, how I found them witless and gave them the use of their wits and made them masters of their minds. I will tell you this, not because I would blame men but to explain the goodwill of my gift. For men at first had eyes, but saw to no purpose; they had ears but did not hear. Like the shapes of dreams they dragged through their long lives and handled all things in bewilderment and confusion. They did not know of building houses with bricks to face the sun, they did not know how to work in wood. They lived like swarming ants in holes in the ground, in the sunless caves of the earth. For them there was no secure token by which to tell winter nor the flowering spring nor the summer with its crops; all their doings were indeed without intelligent calculation until I showed them the rising of the stars, and the settings, hard to observe. And further I discovered to them numbering, preeminent among subtle devices, and the combining of letters as a means of remembering all things, the Muses' mother, skilled in craft. It was I who first yoked beasts for them in the yokes and made of those beasts the slaves of trace chain and pack saddle that they might be man's substitute in the hardest tasks; and I harnessed to the carriage, so that they loved the rein, horses, the crowning pride of the rich man's luxury. It was I and none other who discovered ships, the sail-driven wagons that the sea buffets. Such were the contrivances that I discovered for men—alas for me! For I myself am without contrivance to rid myself of my present affliction.

CHORUS

What you have suffered is indeed terrible. You are all astray and bewildered in your mind and like a bad doctor that has fallen sick himself you are cast down and cannot find what sort of drugs would cure your ailment.

PROMETHEUS

Hear the rest, and you will marvel even more, at the crafts and resources I contrived. Greatest was this: in the former times if a man fell sick he had no defence against the sickness, neither healing food nor drink, nor unguent, but through the lack of drugs men wasted away, until I showed them the blending of mild simples wherewith they drive out all manner of diseases. It was I who arranged all the ways of seercraft and I first adjudged what things come verily true from dreams; and to men I gave meaning to the ominous cries, hard to interpret. It was I who set in order the omens of the highway and the flight of crooked-taloned birds, which of them were propitious or lucky by nature, and what manner of life each led, and what were their mutual hates, loves and companionships; also I taught of the smoothness of the vitals and what color they should have to pleasure the Gods and the dappled beauty of the gall and the lobe. It was I who burnt thighs wrapped in fat and the long shank bone and set mortals on the road to this murky craft. It was I who made visible to men's eyes the flaming signs of the sky that were before dim. So much for these. Beneath the earth, man's hidden blessing, copper, iron, silver and gold—will anyone claim to have discovered these before I did? No one, I am very sure, who wants to speak truly and to the purpose. One brief word will tell the whole story: all arts that mortals have come from Prometheus.

CHORUS

Therefore do not help mortals beyond all expediency while neglecting yourself in your troubles. For I am of good hope that once freed of these bonds you will be no less in power than Zeus.

PROMETHEUS

Not yet has fate that brings to fulfilment determined these things to be thus. I must be twisted by ten thousand pangs and agonies, as I now am, to escape my chains at last. Craft is far weaker than necessity.

CHORUS

Who then is the steersman of necessity?

PROMETHEUS

The triple formed Fates and the remembering Furies.

CHORUS

Is Zeus weaker than these?

PROMETHEUS

Yes, for he, too, cannot escape what is fated.

CHORUS

What is fated for Zeus besides eternal sovereignty?

PROMETHEUS

Inquire of this no further, do not entreat me.

CHORUS

This is some solemn secret, I suppose, that you are hiding.

PROMETHEUS

Think of some other story: this one it is not yet the season to give tongue to, but it must be hidden with all care; for it is only by keeping it that I will escape my despiteful bondage and my agony.

CHORUS

Strophe

May Zeus never, Zeus that all
the universe controls, oppose
his power against my mind:
may I never dallying
be slow to give my worship at
the sacrificial feasts
when the bulls are killed beside
quenchless Father Ocean:
may I never sin in word:
may these precepts still abide
in my mind nor melt away.

Antistrophe

It is a sweet thing to draw out
a long long life in cheerful hopes,
and feed the spirit in the bright
benignity of happiness:
but I shiver when I see you
wasted with ten thousand pains,
all because you did not tremble
at the name of Zeus: your mind
was yours, not his, and at its bidding
you regarded mortal men
too high, Prometheus.

Strophe

Kindness that cannot be requited, tell me,
where is the help in that, my friend? What succor
in creatures of a day? You did not see
the feebleness that draws its breath in gasps,
a dreamlike feebleness by which the race
of man is held in bondage, a blind prisoner.
So the plans of men shall never
pass the ordered law of Zeus.

Antistrophe

This I have learned while I looked on your pains,
deadly pains, Prometheus.

A dirge for you came to my lips, so different
from the other song I sang to crown your marriage
in honor of your couching and your bath,
upon the day you won her with your gifts
to share your bed—of your own race she was,
Hesione—and so you brought her home.

Io

What land is this? what race of men? Who is it
I see here tortured in this rocky bondage?
What is the sin he's paying for? O tell me
to what part of the world my wanderings have brought me.

O, O, O,
there it is again, there again—it stings me,
the gadfly: the ghost of earth-born Argos:
keep it away, keep it away, earth!
I'm frightened when I see the shape of Argos,
Argos the herdsman with ten thousand eyes.
He stalks me with his crafty eyes: he died
but the earth didn't hide him, still he comes
even from the depths of the Underworld to hunt me:
he drives me starving by the sands of the sea.

The reed woven pipe drones on in a hum
and drones and drones its sleep giving strain:
O, O, O,
Where are you bringing me, my far wandering wanderings?
Son of Kronos, what fault, what fault
did you find in me that you should yoke me
to a harness of misery like this,
that you should torture me so to madness
driven in fear of the gadfly?
Burn me with fire: hide me in earth: cast me away
to monsters of the deep for food: but do not
grudge me the granting of this prayer, king.
Enough have my much wandering wanderings
exercised me: I cannot find
a way to escape my troubles.
Do you hear the voice of the cow-horned maid?

PROMETHEUS

Surely I hear the voice, the voice of the maiden, gadfly-haunted, the daughter of Inachus? She set Zeus' heart on fire with love and now she is violently exercised running in courses overlong, driven by Hera's hate.

IO

How is it you speak my father's name?
Tell me, who are you? Who are you? O
who are you that so exactly accosts me by name?
You have spoken of the disease that the Gods have sent to me
which wastes me away, pricking with goads,
so that I am moving always
tortured and hungry, wild bounding,
quick sped I come,
a victim of jealous plots.
Some have been wretched
before me but who of these
suffered as I do?
But declare to me clearly
what I have still to suffer: what would avail
against my sickness, what drug would cure it:
tell me, if you know:
tell me, declare it to the unlucky-wandering maid.

PROMETHEUS

I shall tell you clearly all that you would know, weaving you no riddles, but in plain words, as it is just to open the lips to friends. You see before you him that gave fire to men, even Prometheus.

IO

O spirit that has appeared as a common blessing to all men, unhappy Prometheus, why are you being punished?

PROMETHEUS

I have just this moment ceased from the lamentable tale of my sorrows

Io

Will you then grant me this favor?

PROMETHEUS

Say what you are asking for: I will tell you all.

Io

Tell who it was that nailed you to the cliff.

PROMETHEUS

The plan was the plan of Zeus, and the hand the hand of Hephaestus.

Io

And what was the offense of which this is the punishment?

PROMETHEUS

It is enough that I have told you a clear story so far.

Io

In addition, then, indicate to me what date shall be the limit of my wanderings.

PROMETHEUS

Better for you not to know this than know it.

Io

I beg you, do not hide from me what I must endure.

PROMETHEUS

It is not that I grudge you this favor.

Io

Why then delay to tell me all?

PROMETHEUS

It is no grudging but I hesitate to break your spirit.

Io

Do not have more thought for me than pleases me myself.

PROMETHEUS

Since you are so eager, I must speak; and do you give ear.

CHORUS

Not yet: give me, too, a share of pleasure. First let us question her concerning her sickness, and let her tell us of her desperate fortunes. And then let you be our informant for the sorrows that still await her.

PROMETHEUS

It is your task, Io, to gratify these spirits, for besides other considerations they are your father's sisters. To make wail and lament for one's ill fortune, when one will win a tear from the audience, is well worth while.

IO

I know not how I should distrust you: clearly
you shall hear all you want to know from me.
Yet even as I speak I groan in bitterness
for that storm, sent by God on me, that ruin
of my beauty; I must sorrow when I think
who sent all this upon me. There were always
night visions that kept haunting me and coming
into my maiden chamber and exhorting
with winning words "O maiden greatly blessed,
why are you still a maiden, you who might
make marriage with the greatest? Zeus is stricken
with lust for you, he is afire to try
the bed of love with you: do not disdain him.
Go, child, to Lerna's meadow, deep in grass,
to where your father's flocks and cattle stand
that Zeus' eye may cease from longing for you."
With such dreams I was cruelly beset
night after night until I took the courage
to tell my father of my nightly terror.
He sent to Pytho many an embassy
and to Dodona seeking to discover
what deed or word of his might please the God,

but those he sent came back with riddling oracles
dark and beyond the power of understanding.
At last the word came clear to Inachus
charging him plainly that he cast me out
of home and country, drive me out footloose
to wander to the limits of the world;
if he should not obey, the oracle said,
the fire-faced thunderbolt would come from Zeus
and blot out his whole race. These were the oracles
of Loxias and Inachus obeyed them.
He drove me out and shut his doors against me
with tears on both our parts, but Zeus' bit
compelled him to do this against his will.
Immediately my form and mind were changed
and all distorted; horned, as you see,
pricked on by the sharp biting gadfly, leaping
in frenzied jumps I ran beside the river
Kerchneia, good to drink, and Lerna's spring.
The earth-born herdsman Argos followed me
whose anger knew no limits, and he spied
after my tracks with all his hundred eyes.
Then an unlooked for doom, descending suddenly,
took him from life: I, driven by the gadfly,
that god-sent scourge, was driven always onward
from one land to another: that is my story.
If you can tell me what remains for me,
tell me, and do not out of pity cozen
with kindly lies: there is no sickness worse
for me than words that to be kind must lie.

CHORUS

Hold! Keep away! alas!
never did I think that such strange
words would come to my ears:
never did I think such intolerable
sufferings, an offense to the eye,
shameful and frightening, so
would chill my soul with a double-edged point.

alas, alas, for your fate!
I shudder when I look on Io's fortune.

PROMETHEUS

You groan too soon: you are full of fear too soon: wait till
you hear besides what is to be.

CHORUS

Speak, tell us to the end. For sufferers it is sweet to know
beforehand clearly the pain that still remains for them.

PROMETHEUS

The first request you made of me you gained
lightly: from her you wished to hear the story
of what she suffered. Now hear what remains
what sufferings this maid must yet endure
from Hera. Do you listen, child of Inachus,
hear and lay up my words within your heart
that you may know the limits of your journey.
First turn to the sun's rising and walk on
over the fields no plough has broken: then
you will come to the wandering Scythians
who live in wicker houses built above
their well-wheeled wagons; they are an armed people,
armed with the bow that strikes from far away:
do not draw near them, rather let your feet
touch the surf line of the sea where the waves moan,
and cross their country: on your left there live
the Chalybes who work with iron: these
you must beware of; for they are not gentle,
nor people whom a stranger dare approach.
Then you will come to Insolence, a river
that well deserves its name: but cross it not—
it is no stream that you can easily ford—
until you come to Caucasus itself,
the highest mountains, where the river's strength
gushes from its very temples. Cross these peaks,
the neighbors of the stars, and take the road

southwards until you reach the Amazons,
the race of women who hate men, who one day
shall live around Thermydon in Themiscyra
where Salmydessos, rocky jaw of the sea,
stands sailor hating, stepmother of ships.
The Amazons will set you on your way
and gladly: you will reach Cimmeria,
the isthmus, at the narrow gates of the lake.
Leave this with a good heart and cross the channel,
the channel of Maeotis: and hereafter
for all time men shall talk about your crossing
and they shall call the place for you Cow's-ford.[1]
Leave Europe's mainland then, and go to Asia.

(To the Chorus)

Do you now think this tyrant of the Gods
is hard in all things without difference?
He was a God and sought to lie in love
with this girl who was mortal, and on her
he brought this curse of wandering: bitter indeed
you found your marriage with this suitor, maid.
Yet you must think of all that I have told you
as still only in prelude.

Io

O, O

PROMETHEUS

Again, you are crying and lamenting: what will you do
when you hear of the evils to come?

CHORUS

Is there still something else to her sufferings of which you
will speak?

PROMETHEUS

A wintry sea of agony and ruin.

[1] Cow's-ford: Bosporus.

Io

What good is life to me then? Why do I not throw myself at once from some rough crag, to strike the ground and win a quittance of all my troubles? It would be better to die once for all than suffer all one's days.

PROMETHEUS

You would ill bear my trials, then, for whom Fate reserves no death. Death would be a quittance of trouble: but for me there is no limit of suffering set till Zeus fall from power.

Io

Can Zeus ever fall from power?

PROMETHEUS

You would be glad to see that catastrophe, I think.

Io

Surely, since Zeus is my persecutor.

PROMETHEUS

Then know that this shall be.

Io

Who will despoil him of his sovereign sceptre?

PROMETHEUS

His own witless plans.

Io

How? Tell me, if there is no harm to telling.

PROMETHEUS

He shall make a marriage that shall hurt him.

Io

With god or mortal? Tell me, if you may say it.

PROMETHEUS

Why ask what marriage? That is not to be spoken.

Io

Is it his wife shall cast him from his throne?

PROMETHEUS

She shall bear him a son mightier than his father.

Io

Has he no possibility of escaping this downfall?

PROMETHEUS

None, save through my release from these chains.

Io

But who will free you, against Zeus' will?

PROMETHEUS

Fate has determined that it be one of your descendants.

Io

What, shall a child of mine bring you free?

PROMETHEUS

Yes, in the thirteenth generation.

Io

Your prophesy has now passed the limits of understanding.

PROMETHEUS

Then also do not seek to learn your trials.

Io

Do not offer me a boon and then withhold it.

PROMETHEUS

I offer you then one of two stories.

Io

Which? Tell me and give me the choice.

PROMETHEUS

I will: choose that I tell you clearly either what remains for
you or the one that shall deliver me.

CHORUS

Grant her one and grant me the other and do not deny us
the tale. Tell her what remains of her wanderings: tell us of
the one that shall deliver you. That is what I desire.

PROMETHEUS

Since you have so much eagerness, I will not
refuse to tell you all that you have asked me.
First to you, Io, I shall tell the tale
of your sad wanderings, rich in groans—inscribe
the story in the tablets of your mind.
When you shall cross the channel that divides
Europe from Asia, turn to the rising sun
to the burnt plains, sun-scorched; cross by the edge
of the foaming sea till you come to Gorgona
to the flat stretches of Kisthene's country.
There live the ancient maids, children of Phorcys:
these swan-formed hags, with but one common eye,
single-toothed monsters, such as no where else
the sun's rays look on nor the moon by night.
Near are their winged sisters, the three Gorgons,
with snakes to bind their hair up, mortal hating:
no mortal that but looks on them shall live:
these are the sentry guards I tell you of.
Hear, too, of yet another gruesome sight,
the sharp-toothed hounds of Zeus, that have no bark,
the vultures—them take heed of—and the host
of one-eyed Arimaspians, horse-riding,
that live around the spring which flows with gold,
the spring of Pluto's river: go not near them.
A land far off, a nation of black men,
these you shall come to, men who live hard by
the fountains of the sun where is the river
Aethiops—travel by his banks along
to a waterfall where from the Bibline hills
Nile pours his holy waters, pure to drink.
This river shall be your guide to the triangular
land of the Nile and there, by Fate's decree,

there, Io, you shall found your distant home,
a colony for you and your descendants.
If anything of this is still obscure
or difficult, ask me again and learn
clearly: I have more leisure than I wish.

CHORUS

If there is still something left for you to tell her of her ruinous
wanderings, tell it; but if you have said everything, grant us
the favor we asked and tell us the story too.

PROMETHEUS

The limit of her wanderings complete
she now has heard: but so that she may know
that she has not been listening to no purpose
I shall recount what she endured before
she came to us here: this I give as pledge,
a witness to the good faith of my words.
The great part of the story I omit
and come to the very boundary of your travels.
When you had come to the Molossian plains
around the sheer back of Dodona where
is the oracular seat of Zeus Thesprotian,
the talking oaks, a wonder past belief,
by them full clearly, in no riddling terms,
you were hailed glorious wife of Zeus that shall be:
does anything of this wake pleasant memories?
Then goaded by the gadfly on you hastened
to the great gulf of Rhea by the track
at the side of the sea: but in returning course
you were storm driven back: in time to come
that inlet of the sea shall bear your name
and shall be called Ionian, a memorial
to all men of your journeying: these are proofs
for you, of how my mind sees something farther
than what is visible: for what is left,
to you and you this I shall say in common,
taking up again the track of my old tale.

There is a city, furthest in the world,
Canobos, near the mouth and issuing point
of the Nile: there Zeus shall make you sound of mind
touching you with a hand that brings no fear,
and through that touch alone shall come your healing.
You shall bear Epaphos, dark of skin, his name
recalling Zeus' touch and his begetting.
This Epaphos shall reap the fruit of all
the land that is watered by the broad flowing Nile.
From him five generations, and again
to Argos they shall come, against their will,
in number fifty, women, flying from
a marriage with their kinsfolk: but these kinsfolk
their hearts with lust aflutter like the hawks
barely outdistanced by the doves, will come
hunting a marriage that the law forbids:
the God shall grudge the men these women's bodies:
and the Pelasgian earth shall welcome them
in death: for death shall claim them in a fight
where women strike in the dark, a murderous vigil.
Each wife shall rob her husband of his life
dipping in blood her two-edged sword: even so
may Love come, too, upon my enemies.
But one among these girls shall love beguile
from killing her bedfellow, blunting her purpose:
and she shall make her choice—to bear the name
of coward and not murderer: this girl,
she shall in Argos bear a race of kings.
To tell this clearly needs a longer story,
but from her seed shall spring a man renowned
for archery and he shall set me free.
Such was the prophecy which ancient Themis
my Titan mother opened up to me;
but how and by what means it shall come true
would take too long to tell, and if you heard
the knowledge would not profit you.

Io

Eleleu, eleleu
It creeps on me again, the twitching spasm,
the mind destroying madness, burning me up
and the gadfly's sting goads me on—
steel point by no fire tempered—
and my heart in its fear knocks on my breast.
There's a dazing whirl in my eyes as I run
out of my course by the madness driven,
the crazy frenzy; my tongue ungoverned
babbles, the words in a muddy flow strike
on the waves of the mischief I hate, strike wild
without aim or sense.

Chorus

Strophe

A wise man indeed he was
that first in judgment weighed this word
and gave it tongue: the best by far
it is to marry in one's rank and station:
let no one working with her hands aspire
to marriage with those lifted high in pride
because of wealth, or of ancestral glory.

Antistrophe

Never, never may you see me,
Fates majestic, drawing nigh
the bed of Zeus, to share it with the king:
nor ever may I know a heavenly wooer:
I dread such things beholding
Io's sad virginity
ravaged, ruined; bitter wandering
hers because of Hera's wrath.

Epode

When a match has equal partners
then I fear not: may the eye
inescapable of the mighty

Gods not look on me.
That is a fight that none can fight: a fruitful
source of fruitlessness: I would not
know what I could do: I cannot
see the hope when Zeus is angry
of escaping him.

PROMETHEUS

Yet shall this Zeus, for all his pride of heart
be humble yet: such is the match he plans,
a marriage that shall drive him from his power
and from his throne, out of the sight of all.
So shall at last the final consummation
be brought about of Father Kronos' curse
which he, driven from his ancient throne, invoked
against the son deposing him: no one
of all the Gods save I alone can tell
a way to escape this mischief: I alone
know it and how. So let him confidently
sit on his throne and trust his heavenly thunder
and brandish in his hand his fiery bolt.
Nothing shall all of this avail against
a fall intolerable, a dishonoured end,
so strong a wrestler Zeus is now equipping
against himself, a monster hard to fight.
This enemy shall find a plan to best
the thunderbolt, a thunderclap to best
the thunderclap of Zeus: and he shall shiver
Poseidon's trident, curse of sea and land.
So, in his crashing fall shall Zeus discover
how different are rule and slavery.

CHORUS

You voice your wishes for the God's destruction.

PROMETHEUS

They are my wishes, yet shall come to pass.

CHORUS

Must we expect some one to conquer Zeus?

PROMETHEUS
Yes; he shall suffer worse than I do now.

CHORUS
Have you no fear of uttering such words?

PROMETHEUS
Why should I fear, since death is not my fate?

CHORUS
But he might give you pain still worse than this.

PROMETHEUS
Then let him do so; all this I expect.

CHORUS
Wise are the worshippers of Adrasteia.

PROMETHEUS
Worship him, pray; flatter whatever king
is king today; but I care less than nothing
for Zeus. Let him do what he likes,
let him be king for his short time: he shall not
be king for long.
       Look, here is Zeus' footman,
this fetch-and-carry messenger of him,
the New King. Certainly he has come here
with news for us.

HERMES
       You, subtle-spirit, you
bitterly overbitter, you that sinned
against the immortals, giving honor to
the creatures of a day, you thief of fire:
the Father has commanded you to say
what marriage of his is this you brag about
that shall drive him from power,—and declare it
in clear terms and no riddles. You, Prometheus,
do not cause me a double journey; these (*pointing to the chains*)
will prove to you that Zeus is not soft-hearted.

PROMETHEUS

Your speech is pompous sounding, full of pride,
as fits the lackey of the Gods. You are young
and young your rule and you think that the tower
in which you live is free of sorrow: from it
have I not seen two tyrants thrown? the third,
who now is king, I shall yet live to see him
fall, of all three most suddenly, most dishonoured.
Do you think I will crouch before your Gods,
—so new—and tremble? I am far from that.
Hasten away, back on the road you came.
You shall learn nothing that you ask of me.

HERMES

Just such the obstinacy that brought you here,
to this self-willed calamitous anchorage.

PROMETHEUS

Be sure of this: when I set my misfortune
against your slavery, I would not change.

HERMES

It is better, I suppose, to be a slave
to this rock, than Zeus' trusted messenger.

PROMETHEUS

Thus must the insolent show their insolence!

HERMES

I think you find your present lot too soft.

PROMETHEUS

Too soft? I would my enemies had it then,
and you are one of those I count as such.

HERMES

O, you would blame me too for your calamity?

PROMETHEUS

In a single word, I am the enemy
of all the Gods that gave me ill for good.

HERMES
Your words declare you mad, and mad indeed.

PROMETHEUS
Yes, if it's madness to detest my foes.

HERMES
No one could bear you in success.

PROMETHEUS
                              Alas!

HERMES
Alas! *Zeus* does not know that word.

PROMETHEUS
Time in its ageing course teaches all things.

HERMES
But you have not yet learned a wise discretion.

PROMETHEUS
True: or I would not speak so to a servant.

HERMES
It seems you will not grant the Father's wish.

PROMETHEUS
I should be glad, indeed, to requite his kindness!

HERMES
You mock me like a child!

PROMETHEUS
                    and are you not
a child, and sillier than a child, to think
that I should tell you anything? There is not
a torture or an engine wherewithal
Zeus can induce me to declare these things,
till he has loosed me from these cruel shackles.
So let him hurl his smoky lightning flame,

and throw in turmoil all things in the world
with white winged snow flakes and deep bellowing
thunder beneath the earth: me he shall not
bend by all this to tell him who is fated
to drive him from his tyranny.

HERMES

Think, here and now, if this seems to your interest.

PROMETHEUS

I have already thought—and laid my plans.

HERMES

Bring your proud heart to know a true discretion—
O foolish spirit—in the face of ruin.

PROMETHEUS

You vex me by these senseless adjurations,
senseless as if you were to advise the waves.
Let it not cross your mind that I will turn
womanish-minded from my fixed decision
or that I shall entreat the one I hate
so greatly, with a woman's upturned hands,
to loose me from my chains: I am far from that.

HERMES

I have said too much already—so I think—
and said it to no purpose: you are not softened:
your purpose is not dented by my prayers.
You are a colt new broken, with the bit
clenched in its teeth, fighting against the reins,
and bolting. You are far too strong and confident
in your weak cleverness. For obstinacy
standing alone is the weakest of all things
in one whose mind is not possessed by wisdom.
Think what a storm, a triple wave of ruin
will rise against you, if you will not hear me,
and no escape for you. First this rough crag
with thunder and the lightning bolt the Father

shall cleave asunder, and shall hide your body
wrapped in a rocky clasp within its depth;
a tedious length of time you must fulfil
before you see the light again, returning.
Then Zeus' winged hound, the eagle red,
shall tear great shreds of flesh from you, a feaster
coming unbidden, every day: your liver
bloodied to blackness will be his repast.
And of this pain do not expect an end
until some God shall show himself successor
to take your tortures for himself and willing
go down to lightless Hades and the shadows
of Tartarus' depths. Bear this in mind
and so determine. This is no feigned boast
but spoken with too much truth. The mouth of Zeus
does not know how to lie, but every word
brings to fulfilment. Look, you, and reflect
and never think that obstinacy is better
than prudent counsel.

CHORUS
            Hermes seems to us
to speak not altogether out of season.
He bids you leave your obstinacy and seek
a wise good counsel. Hearken to him. Shame
it were for one so wise to fall in error.

PROMETHEUS
Before he told it me I knew this message:
but there is no disgrace in suffering
at an enemy's hand, when you hate mutually.
So let the curling tendril of the fire
from the lightning bolt be sent against me: let
the air be stirred with thunderclaps, the winds
in savage blasts convulsing all the world.
Let earth to her foundations shake, yes to her root,
before the quivering storm: let it confuse
the paths of heavenly stars and the sea's waves

in a wild surging torrent: this my body
let Him raise up on high and dash it down
into black Tartarus with rigorous
compulsive eddies: death he cannot give me.

HERMES

These are a madman's words, a madman's plans:
is there a missing note in this mad harmony?
is there a slack chord in his madness? You,
you, who are so sympathetic with his troubles,
away with you from here, quickly away!
lest you should find your wits stunned by the thunder
and its hard deafening roar.

CHORUS

                          say something else
different from this: give me some other counsel
that I will listen to: this word of yours
for all its instancy is not for us.
How dare you bid us practise baseness? we
will bear along with him what we must bear.
I have learned to hate all traitors: there is no
disease I spit on more than treachery.

HERMES

Remember then my warning before the act:
when you are trapped by ruin don't blame fortune:
don't say that Zeus has brought you to calamity
that you could not foresee: do not do this:
but blame yourselves: now you know what you're doing:
and with this knowledge neither suddenly
nor secretly your own want of good sense
has tangled you in the net of ruin, past
all hope of rescue.

PROMETHEUS

Now it is words no longer: now in very truth
the earth is staggered: in its depths the thunder

bellows resoundingly, the fiery tendrils
of the lightning flash light up, and whirling clouds
carry the dust along: all the winds' blasts
dance in a fury one against the other
in violent confusion: earth and sea
are one, confused together: such is the storm
that comes against me manifestly from Zeus
to work its terrors. Holy mother mine,
Sun that drives round in circles light for all,
you see me, how I suffer, how unjustly.

SOPHOCLES: *OEDIPUS THE KING*

INTRODUCTION

THE *Oedipus* has, perhaps too frequently, been called a tragedy of destiny. It is not that such an appellation is undeserved; certainly, we are conscious from the beginning of the action in *Oedipus* of its inevitable outcome. In hardly any other play are we so constantly aware of the struggle between a man and something stronger than a man. It is precisely this which awakens in us a fascinated horror as we watch his struggles and finally grasp the bitter irony of the situation—that it is Oedipus' own efforts to escape his fate which draw him nearer and nearer to it. Yet to call the *Oedipus* a tragedy of destiny is perhaps to call up with that title a mass of associations which do not belong here. Very often we interpret "tragedy of destiny" to mean the struggle of a man against a clearly seen adversary of greater strength than he, which he nonetheless fights, in spite of his knowledge of ultimate defeat. This is not the plot of the *Oedipus*. The excellence which the play possesses lies precisely in the odd and even of chance which control the most significant developments of the action. Viewed from one angle, the *Oedipus* might be described as a psychological mystery story, in which the clues arise from the most trivial and accidental circumstances.

As we examine the closely woven texture of this play, we become aware of three starting-points for new development in the action, none of which springs from any conscious intention on the part of the king. First, there is the plague and the natural consultation of the oracle and the pronouncement of the oracle to the effect that the cause of the plague is the pollution of an unavenged murder. It is not often stressed as much as it should be that the plague is a compelling force throughout the whole course of the action. There have been commentators who have tried to trace all the developments to Oedipus' impetuosity in pressing on the search for the murderer. This is to neglect the important fact that, come what may, Oedipus *must*, as king and patriotic Theban, rid the country of the sickness which was devouring it. There is no going back upon that road. Whether or not in the last stages of that investigation Oedipus was really more interested in his own fate than in the city's, whether or not the general happiness or misery of his people had narrowed to the prospects of his own personal happiness or misery, is not an important question. Oedipus as king of Thebes *must* find the murderer, even if that murderer is himself, unless he is to bring his state to that sad condition of which the priest speaks: "for neither town nor ship is anything/when empty and none live in it together." Thus, when under the pressure of the plague Oedipus consults the oracle, receives its answer, and makes public proclamation of a curse upon the murderer, he is merely doing what any right-minded king would do. But he is also slamming the door upon the possibility of his retreat. And Sophocles makes just that point in the end of the play when Oedipus, in indicating the hopelessness of his position, says that under no circumstances may he remain in Thebes to prolong the pestilence among his own people.

The second starting-point of significant action (and the first of the two major clues to the mystery) is the chance mention of crossroads by Jocasta. It is the most arresting feature of Sophocles' irony that, as the word "crossroads" seizes Oedipus' attention and holds him in terrified suspense, he should fail to notice the much more overt reference to the baby exposed with pierced ankles. Later, in the Shepherd's revelation, the pierced ankles are to be the final proof in the chain, the riveting of certainty in the mind of Oedipus. But exactly the same clue is given at this early stage of the story, and he passes it over because he is concentrated upon the relatively minor issue awakened by the tale of the man who was killed at the crossroads. It is a further example of Sophocles' irony that the ultimate identification of Oedipus with the alleged highwayman who killed

Laius at the crossroads is never made. When the old herdsman is summoned, expressly to clear up this mystery, the
king puts no question to him on this head. By that time his
whole attention is engrossed by the major mystery of his
birth. When this is solved, the weight of the original prediction of the oracle—that he should kill his father and marry
his mother—convinces him that he was also the murderer of
Laius and makes any further interrogation of the herdsman
pointless. But it is characteristic of Sophocles' method in
this play to make the starting-point of Oedipus' investigation finally unimportant in the solution and to reveal the
king as missing at the outset the much more obvious clue to
the major mystery. Perhaps, however, there is no more re-
markable case of how circumstances make the insignificant
and obscure seem significant and the important and obvious
seem insignificant than the juxtaposition of Oedipus' conversation with Teiresias and his subsequent talk with Jocasta, in which his ear is caught by the sound of the word
"crossroads." The prophet tells him in no uncertain terms
that he, the king, is actually the murderer of Laius and consequently the cause of the pollution of his country, and he
predicts exactly what the outcome of Oedipus' search will
be. Jocasta merely mentions to Oedipus the small fact that
Laius was killed at a crossroads. But Sophocles has spent a
great deal of pains on making us see, if we choose, *why*
Oedipus is not only completely incredulous of Teiresias'
story but very suspicious of the integrity of the prophet himself. Oedipus, in accordance with the oracle's instructions,
is looking for the murderer of his predecessor; and it never
enters his mind, naturally enough, that that murderer might
have been in ignorance of the identity of the man he murdered. In fact, as he says to Creon, there is a strong presumption that the murder was the result of a political plot
hatched in Thebes itself. All that rumor had to say about
the matter was that certain highwaymen had killed the
former king when he was on a journey. It would hardly
seem reasonable to Oedipus to infer at once that the highwaymen who waylaid the king of Thebes did not know

whom they were in wait for. On the other hand, Jocasta's reference to a man killed at a crossroads awakens Oedipus' own recollection of an episode many years old. In that case he is not asked to identify himself at once with the murderer of Laius; but a single detail of Laius' murder recalls his own experience and leads him indirectly to the fear that that experience was the occasion of Laius' murder. While Teiresias' accusation that Oedipus was Laius' murderer, elaborated with detail, had seemed so utterly impossible to the king that the only explanation was Teiresias' duplicity, the trivial instance of the location of the murder carries almost instant conviction. But Sophocles has given us a further example of brilliant subtlety of implication. Why is Oedipus so ready to believe that Teiresias is dishonest? Well, if one views the prophet as the spokesman of Apollo and, forgetting the traditional Greek view of seers, one makes of Teiresias a compound of a modern archbishop and an Old Testament prophet, the king's conduct indeed seems very stupid, not to say reprehensible. But a careful reading of the play and some understanding of the Greek attitude toward various aspects of organized religion, produce a very different effect. Teiresias was a professional prophet who had failed to solve the Sphinx's riddle—which Oedipus, the amateur, the adventurer, had solved. The seer might, therefore, quite reasonably be expected to bear him a grudge. And Teiresias was sent for on the express advice of Creon, who was next heir to the throne, and heir in virtue of a traditional legitimacy to which Oedipus could never lay claim. What could be more natural for Oedipus than to suppose that the two conventional representatives—the one of priesthood and the other of royalty—had conspired together to remove this parvenu, whose seership and whose kingship was an insult to both? As to the most widespread distrust of the honesty of oracles among the Greeks, nothing could be more substantiated from ancient literature. Even that fairly orthodox religionist, Herodotus, has the gravest doubts of the integrity of almost two-thirds of the oracles quoted in the histories; and Thucydides, Euripides, and the later writers can be cited broadcast for a general national Greek suspicion that, if sometimes the oracles, including Apollo at Delphi, spoke with the words of God, there were many, many times they spoke the words of men who had paid them well for so doing.

The third starting-point of important action in the *Oedipus*, which again springs from no conscious intention and certainly no blameworthy defect in Oedipus, is the gratuitous information supplied him by the messenger from Corinth, to the effect that Polybus and Merope were not his parents. To tell this was no part of the messenger's intention when he came. It was one of those chance inspirations provoked by Oedipus' seemingly irrational reluctance to return to Corinth in the face of the old oracle about his parents. But it is exactly this gratuitous bit of information which sets Oedipus on the last stage of the road to his own doom. It leads him back to the herdsman who was already involved in the crossroads clue, and in a trice the whole horrible truth is clear.

Now, it seems to me, the importance of the accidental quality of the significant clues cannot be too much insisted on. It is, says Sophocles, the trivial and the accidental which precipitated the horrible fate which has hung over this man's head for fifteen or more years. And he emphasizes the trivial and accidental nature of the clues by showing us Oedipus as quite naturally impervious to the frontal assault of the major clues, whose obviousness strikes the reader even to the point of irritation. Yet, if you can remove from yourself the ingrained knowledge of the main outlines of this plot, the mental processes of Oedipus prove to be correctly and profoundly studied. In the ultimate release of the long-threatening doom it is not the direct and obvious provocations which are effectual but the indirect, insidious, and accidental impingement of details which carry an inner conviction.

In view of the preceding account of the development of the play, it may be pertinently asked: What is the significance of Oedipus' scene with Teiresias and Oedipus' scene with Creon, both of them at the beginning of the action before the train has been started in the solution of the mystery itself? If all the important starting-points in the plot are the chance incidents, the forces extraneous to Oedipus himself, why should there be these two scenes, both of which may be said to emphasize Oedipus' injustice (whether pardonable or otherwise) and both of which plainly emphasize the theme of the proud man riding for a fall?

It may be illuminating, in answering such a question, first to indicate what Oedipus' treatment of Teiresias or Oedipus' treatment of Creon does *not* mean in terms of the progression of the action. Had Oedipus reverently acquiesced in the warning of Teiresias, we ask ourselves, what would have been the outcome? First, notice that Teiresias' denunciation of Oedipus as the criminal who is sought is not given spontaneously or initially but solely after Oedipus' goading and insinuation. Had the prophet not lost his temper (and perhaps Jebb is right to point out that it is hardly worthy of such a prophet to lose his temper and hardly worthy to utter such taunts as Teiresias does), there would have been no explicit prophecy of the things that were to come for both Oedipus and Thebes in the search for Laius' murderer. So we are left to ask ourselves: What had the prophet to say to Oedipus when he came to him? What advice had he to give him which a more pious or less impetuous king would have heeded? The answer is to give up the search for the murderer. That is actually what the prophet says: "Don't try to find out who he is. I, who know, won't tell you, and it's better for you not to trouble about this." But this advice is exactly that which the king cannot follow, even allowing that it would be honorable for him to do so. Because, as long as the plague remains a factor in the situation, Oedipus has to look for the murderer, unless he is ready to live and be king in an empty city. And Teiresias realizes that the truth is bound to come out in that search, irrespective of whether he tells Oedipus or not, and he says that. So Teiresias' denunciation of Oedipus is not a solemn warning which the king disregards to his own hurt, but a revelation of what is to come, which pierces the obscurity and confusion of the situation like a lightning flash only to vanish again and leave Oedipus and the Chorus groping in uncertainty as to its meaning. But for the total effect upon the audience this lightning flash is of immense psychological importance. It would be rash to assume that very many of those who saw the play in the Theater of Dionysus were ignorant of the outlines of the plot, though some such there probably were. However, it is not to illuminate complete ignorance that the speech of Teiresias is intended but to keep in the minds of audience or reader the truth which is lurking back of the search for Laius' murderer, the truth which peers out obscurely at each turn in the play's course. The tragedy of the Greeks partakes very constantly of this quality. It is played out between certainty and doubt, between the certainty in general concerning the outcome and the ignorance of the exact form of that outcome. Without Teiresias' flash of anger and his blind vision of the future, there would be nothing to hold the whole play together; there would be no backdrop of certain danger against which we see every phase of Oedipus' search develop.

Slightly different is the case of the scene between Oedipus and Creon. It underlines the injustice which Oedipus is naturally impelled to commit—an injustice because Creon, by Oedipus' own admission, is a man who has been constantly loyal to him from the beginning. It is the high-water mark of the pride and strength of the king of Thebes, that he may condemn the queen's brother for a presumptive offense against himself. Creon is Kent to Oedipus' Lear. In both Lear and Oedipus there is a great blindness of the world in which they live and move; and, in virtue of that blindness, while we resent, we can understand and even pardon their injustice. And both Creon and Kent are to be used at the ends of their respective tragedies to mark how low their two kings have fallen. The Kent whom Lear could banish at the height of his power for a slight criticism is the sole loyal adherent of the crazy old tottering beggar of the play's end; the Creon whose life or death lies in the word of Oedipus, whose life is obtained from the king only by entreaty of Jocasta and the Chorus, is the Creon whose sovereign power in the conclusion will grant the blinded Oedipus the only favor which means anything to him, the embrace of his daughters. These two scenes—that with Teiresias and that with Creon—have a strong contrapuntal effect in their contrast with the play's end. The prophet that was blind saw, and the king that saw was blind. The traitor who was banished on mere suspicion by his all-powerful lord is the king who can dispose of the destiny of his humiliated former ruler. But it must be said once again, in terms of the play's action, nothing whatever is generated out of Oedipus' quarrel either with Teiresias or with Creon. Neither Teiresias' warning nor Creon's defense swerves Oedipus from the path he was traveling or speeds him on it any the quicker.

The play, then, the more we study it, becomes a picture of the complexity and chaos of life itself, strangely overridden by a compelling direction of events. There is no black and white of moral values. Oedipus is unjust to both Teiresias and Creon, but it is an injustice which springs from the most natural misconception. The life which Oedipus has lived is sufficiently horrible, even if our feeling about the violation of taboos has not the definitely religious significance it had for the Greeks; but no one can exactly be blamed for that life. It is not even possible to blame the gods, for the oracles, in so far as they are the voice of god, only predicted, not contrived, the havoc. There is no point in the plot at which turning back is possible; and yet all the advances on the path to destruction are taken voluntarily on the stimulation of some chance happening or utterance. The only quality in Oedipus' nature which drives him to this particular form of ending his road of destiny is not particularly a morally reprehensible one. It is his basic insecurity. He is a king, but he has no traditional or conventional claim on anyone's allegiance. He won his kingship by energetic action, when he saved the city from the Sphinx. He must keep his kingship by energetic action in banishing the plague. As the priest says: "So, let us never speak about your reign/as of a time in which at first our feet/were set on high and after fell to ruin." There is no chance for Oedipus ever to relapse into the tranquillity of an eventless reign. As a man of action he won the allegiance of Thebes, as a man of action he must keep it. Oedipus had a reputation for dealing with situations "where mortal has to do with more than man," for he had delivered his city from the Sphinx. But again his skill was the skill of the amateur. The knowledge of his one success provokes him to fling it in Teiresias' face—"You were the professional and I the amateur, but I succeeded when you failed"—yet he has no confidence that he possesses any real understanding of what is "more than man" to help him through a contingency worse than the Sphinx's riddle. He is insecure even in respect to his wife, for neither he nor she knows who he is, and the dim remembrance of the taunt at the dinner table when he was a young man in Corinth flares into new life when he rashly taunts Jocasta with being unable to face the real facts of his birth. Oedipus is a restless, brave, insecure spirit, whom the chance currents of a given situation carry on a course mapped out with what looks like a horrible logic by an amoral and inhuman fate.

There have been many discussions as to the theological significance of Sophocles' *Oedipus*. There have not been wanting those who said that it is a protest against the cruelty of a divine power or those who saw in it the story of a taboo so sacred that even its unconscious violation merits extreme punishment. It does not seem that a careful reading of the play does much to give authority to either of these judgments. Rather, Sophocles has written a story out of a profoundly tragic conception of existence, which envisages the shipwreck of a life through some malicious quirk of fate's logic as it tries to save itself—a destruction brought about by accident and chance, yet controlled by an inexorable planless plan; a tangle of events which has no good reason for beginning or ending but a maddening symmetry and balance. What Sophocles thought of the power that had created such a life and made Oedipus lead it, we may guess or not as we please. But in Sophocles the dramatist, who wrote the play *Oedipus the King*, we will find no answer.

OEDIPUS THE KING

SCENE: *In front of the palace of Oedipus at Thebes. To the right of the stage near the altar stands the Priest with a crowd of children. Oedipus emerges from the central door.*

*   *   *

OEDIPUS

Children, young sons and daughters of old Cadmus,
why do you sit here with your suppliant crowns?
The town is heavy with a mingled burden
of sounds and smells, of groans and hymns and incense;
I did not think it fit that I should hear
of this from messengers but came myself,—
I Oedipus whom all men call the Great.

(He turns to the Priest.)

You're old and they are young; come, speak for them.
What do you fear or want, that you sit here
suppliant? Indeed I'm willing to give all
that you may need; I would be very hard
should I not pity suppliants like these.

PRIEST

O ruler of my country, Oedipus,
you see our company around the altar;
you see our ages; some of us, like these,
who cannot yet fly far, and some of us
heavy with age; these children are the chosen
among the young, and I the priest of Zeus.
Within the market place sit others crowned
with suppliant garlands, at the double shrine
of Pallas and the temple where Ismenus
gives oracles by fire. King, you yourself
have seen our city reeling like a wreck
already; it can scarcely lift its prow

87

out of the depths, out of the bloody surf.
A blight is on the fruitful plants of the earth,
a blight is on the cattle in the fields,
a blight is on our women that no children
are born to them; a God that carries fire,
a deadly pestilence, is on our town,
strikes us and spares not, and the house of Cadmus
is emptied of its people while black Death
grows rich in groaning and in lamentation.
We have not come as suppliants to this altar
because we thought of you as of a God,
but rather judging you the first of men
in all the chances of this life and when
we mortals have to do with more than man.
You came and by your coming saved our city,
freed us from tribute which we paid of old
to the Sphinx, cruel singer. This you did
in virtue of no knowledge we could give you,
in virtue of no teaching; it was God
that aided you, men say, and you are held
with God's assistance to have saved our lives.
Now Oedipus, whom all men call the Greatest,
here falling at your feet we all entreat you,
find us some strength for rescue.
Perhaps you'll hear a wise word from some God,
perhaps you will learn something from a man
(for I have seen that for the skilled of practice
the outcome of their counsels live the most).
Noblest of men, go, and raise up our city,
go,—and give heed. For now this land of ours
calls you its savior since you saved it once.
So, let us never speak about your reign
as of a time when first our feet were set
secure on high, but later fell to ruin.
Raise up our city, save it and raise it up.
Once you have brought us luck with happy omen;
be no less now in fortune.
If you will rule this land, as now you rule it,
better to rule it full of men than empty.

For neither town nor ship is anything
when empty, and none live in it together.

OEDIPUS

Poor children! You have come to me entreating,
but I have known the story before you told it
only too well. I know you are all sick,
yet there is not one of you, sick though you are,
that is as sick as I myself.
Your several sorrows each have single scope
and touch but one of you. My spirit groans
for city and myself and you at once.
You have not roused me like a man from sleep;
know that I have given many tears to this,
gone many ways wandering in thought,
but as I thought I found only one remedy
and that I took. I sent Menoeceus' son
Creon, Jocasta's brother, to Apollo,
to his Pythian temple,
that he might learn there by what act or word
I could save this city. As I count the days,
it vexes me what ails him; he is gone
far longer than he needed for the journey.
But when he comes, then, may I prove a villain,
if I shall not do all the God commands.

PRIEST

Thanks for your gracious words. Your servants here
signal that Creon is this moment coming.

OEDIPUS

His face is bright. O holy Lord Apollo,
grant that his news too may be bright for us
and bring us safety.

PRIEST

It is happy news,
I think, for else his head would not be crowned
with sprigs of fruitful laurel.

OEDIPUS

               We will know soon,
he's within hail. Lord Creon, my good brother,
what is the word you bring us from the God?

               (Creon enters.)

CREON

A good word,—for things hard to bear themselves
if in the final issue all is well
I count complete good fortune.

OEDIPUS

               What do you mean?
What you have said so far
leaves me uncertain whether to trust or fear.

CREON

If you will hear my news before these others
I am ready to speak, or else to go within.

OEDIPUS

Speak it to all;
the grief I bear, I bear it more for these
than for my own heart.

CREON

               I will tell you, then,
what I heard from the God.
King Phoebus in plain words commanded us
to drive out a pollution from our land,
pollution grown ingrained within the land;
drive it out, said the God, not cherish it,
till it's past cure.

OEDIPUS

               What is the rite
of purification? How shall it be done?

CREON

By banishing a man, or expiation
of blood by blood, since it is murder guilt
which holds our city in this storm of death.

OEDIPUS

Who is this man whose fate the God pronounces?

CREON

My Lord, before you piloted the state
we had a king called Laius.

OEDIPUS

I know of him by hearsay. I have not seen him.

CREON

The God commanded clearly: let some one
punish with force this dead man's murderers.

OEDIPUS

Where are they in the world? Where would a trace
of this old crime be found? It would be hard
to guess where.

CREON

               The clue is in this land;
that which is sought is found;
the unheeded thing escapes:
so said the God.

OEDIPUS

                     Was it at home,
or in the country that death came upon him,
or in another country travelling?

CREON

He went, he said himself, upon an embassy,
but never returned when he set out from home.

OEDIPUS

Was there no messenger, no fellow traveller
who knew what happened? Such a one might tell
something of use.

CREON

They were all killed save one. He fled in terror
and he could tell us nothing in clear terms
of what he knew, nothing, but one thing only.

OEDIPUS

What was it?
If we could even find a slim beginning
in which to hope, we might discover much.

CREON

This man said that the robbers they encountered
were many and the hands that did the murder
were many; it was no man's single power.

OEDIPUS

How could a robber dare a deed like this
were he not helped with money from the city,
money and treachery?

CREON

     That indeed was thought.
But Laius was dead and in our trouble
there was none to help.

OEDIPUS

What trouble was so great to hinder you
inquiring out the murder of your king?

CREON

The riddling Sphinx induced us to neglect
mysterious crimes and rather seek solution
of troubles at our feet.

OEDIPUS

I will bring this to light again. King Phoebus
fittingly took this care about the dead,
and you too fittingly.
And justly you will see in me an ally,
a champion of my country and the God.

For when I drive pollution from the land
I will not serve a distant friend's advantage,
but act in my own interest. Whoever
he was that killed the king may readily
wish to dispatch me with his murderous hand;
so helping the dead king I help myself.

Come children, take your suppliant boughs and go;
up from the altars now. Call the assembly
and let it meet upon the understanding
that I'll do everything. God will decide
whether we prosper or remain in sorrow.

PRIEST

Rise, children—it was this we came to seek,
which of himself the king now offers us.
May Phoebus who gave us the oracle
come to our rescue and stay the plague.

(*Exeunt all but the Chorus.*)

CHORUS

Strophe

What is the sweet spoken word of God from the shrine of
    Pytho rich in gold
that has come to glorious Thebes?
I am stretched on the rack of doubt, and terror and trem-
    bling hold
my heart, O Delian Healer, and I worship full of fears
for what doom you will bring to pass, new or renewed in
    the revolving years.
Speak to me, immortal voice,
child of golden Hope.

Antistrophe

First I call on you, Athene, deathless daughter of Zeus,
and Artemis, Earth Upholder,
who sits in the midst of the market place in the throne
    which men call Fame,
and Phoebus, the Far Shooter, three averters of Fate,

come to us now, if ever before, when ruin rushed upon the
    state,
you drove destruction's flame away
out of our land.

Strophe

Our sorrows defy number;
all the ship's timbers are rotten;
taking of thought is no spear for the driving away of the
    plague.
There are no growing children in this famous land;
there are no women staunchly bearing the pangs of child-
    birth.
You may see them one with another, like birds swift on the
    wing,
quicker than fire unmastered,
speeding away to the coast of the Western God.

Antistrophe

In the unnumbered deaths
of its people the city dies;
those children that are born lie dead on the naked earth
unpitied, spreading contagion of death; and grey haired
    mothers and wives
everywhere stand at the altar's edge, suppliant, moaning;
the hymn to the healing God rings out but with it the wailing
    voices are blended.
From these our sufferings grant us, O golden Daughter of
    Zeus,
glad faced deliverance.

Strophe

There is no clash of brazen shields but our fight is with the
    War God,
a War God ringed with the cries of men, a savage God who
    burns us;
grant that he turn in racing course backwards out of our
    country's bounds

to the great palace of Amphitrite or where the waves of the
    Thracian sea
deny the stranger safe anchorage.
Whatsoever escapes the night
at last the light of day revisits;
so smite the War God, Father Zeus,
beneath your thunderbolt,
for you are the Lord of the lightning, the lightning that
carries fire.

Antistrophe

And your unconquered arrow shafts, winged by the golden
    corded bow,
Lycean King, I beg to be at our side for help;
and the gleaming torches of Artemis with which she scours
    the Lycean hills,
and I call on the God with the turban of gold, who gave his
    name to this country of ours,
the Bacchic God with the wine flushed face,
Evian One, who travel
with the Maenad company,
combat the God that burns us
with your torch of pine;
for the God that is our enemy is a God unhonoured among
    the Gods.

           (*Oedipus returns.*)

OEDIPUS

For what you ask me—if you will hear my words,
and hearing welcome them and fight the plague,
you will find strength and lightening of your load.

Hark to me; what I say to you, I say
as one that is a stranger to the story
as stranger to the deed. For I would not
be far upon the track if I alone
were tracing it without a clue. But now,
since after all was finished, I became
a citizen among you, citizens—
now I proclaim to all the men of Thebes:

who so among you knows the murderer
by whose hand Laius, son of Labdacus,
died—I command him to tell everything
to me,—yes, though he fears himself to take the blame
on his own head; for bitter punishment
he shall have none, but leave this land unharmed.
Or if he knows the murderer, another,
a foreigner, still let him speak the truth.
For I will pay him and be grateful, too.
But if you shall keep silence, if perhaps
some one of you, to shield a guilty friend,
or for his own sake shall reject my words—
hear what I shall do then:
I forbid that man, whoever he be, my land,
my land where I hold sovereignty and throne;
and I forbid any to welcome him
or cry him greeting or make him a sharer
in sacrifice or offering to the Gods,
or give him water for his hands to wash.
I command all to drive him from their homes,
since he is our pollution, as the oracle
of Pytho's God proclaimed him now to me.
So I stand forth a champion of the God
and of the man who died.
Upon the murderer I invoke this curse—
whether he is one man and all unknown,
or one of many—may he wear out his life
in misery to miserable doom!
If with my knowledge he lives at my hearth
I pray that I myself may feel my curse.

Even were this no matter of God's ordinance
it would not fit you so to leave it lie,
unpurified, since a good man is dead
and one that was a king. Search it out.
Since I am now the holder of his office,
and have his bed and wife that once was his,
and had his line not been unfortunate

we would have common children—(fortune leaped
upon his head)—because of all these things,
I fight in his defence as for my father,
and I shall try all means to take the murderer
of Laius the son of Labdacus
the son of Polydorus and before him
of Cadmus and before him of Agenor.
Those who do not obey me, may the Gods
grant no crops springing from the ground they plough
nor children to their women! May a fate
like this, or one still worse than this consume them!
For you whom these words please, the other Thebans,
may Justice as your ally and all the Gods
live with you, blessing you now and for ever!

CHORUS

As you have held me to my oath, I speak:
I neither killed the king nor can declare
the killer; but since Phoebus set the quest
it is his part to tell who the man is.

OEDIPUS

Right; but to put compulsion on the Gods
against their will—no man has strength for that.

CHORUS

May I then say what I think second best?

OEDIPUS

If there's a third best, too, spare not to tell it.

CHORUS

I know that what the Lord Teiresias
sees, is most often what the Lord Apollo
sees. If you should inquire of this from him
you might find out most clearly.

OEDIPUS

Even in this my actions have not been sluggard.
On Creon's word I have sent two messengers

and why the prophet is not here already
I have been wondering.

CHORUS

His skill apart
there is besides only an old faint story.

OEDIPUS
What is it?
I seize on every story.

CHORUS

It was said
that he was killed by certain wayfarers.

OEDIPUS
I heard that, too, but no one saw the killer.

CHORUS
Yet if he has a share of fear at all,
his courage will not stand firm, hearing your curse.

OEDIPUS
The man who in the doing did not shrink
will fear no word.

CHORUS

Here comes his prosecutor:
led by your men the godly prophet comes
in whom alone of mankind truth is native.

(*Enter Teiresias, led by a little boy.*)

OEDIPUS
Teiresias, you are versed in everything,
things teachable and things not to be spoken,
things of the heaven and earth-creeping things.
You have no eyes but in your mind you know
with what a plague our city is afflicted.
My lord, in you alone we find a champion,

in you alone one that can rescue us.
Perhaps you have not heard the messengers,
but Phoebus sent in answer to our sending
an oracle declaring that our freedom
from this disease would only come when we
should learn the names of those who killed King Laius,
and kill them or expel from our country.
Do not begrudge us oracles from birds,
or any other way of prophecy
within your skill; save yourself and the city,
save me; redeem the debt of our pollution
that lies on us because of this dead man.
We are in your hands; it is the finest task
to help another when you have means and power.

TEIRESIAS

Alas, how terrible is wisdom when
it brings no profit to the man that's wise!
This I knew well, but had forgotten it.
else I would not have come here.

OEDIPUS

What is this?
How sad you are now you have come!

TEIRESIAS

Let me
go home. It will be easiest for us both
to bear our several destinies to the end
if you will follow my advice.

OEDIPUS

You'd rob us
of this your gift of prophecy? You talk
as one who had no care for law nor love
for Thebes who reared you.

TEIRESIAS

Yes, but I see that even your own words
miss the mark; therefore I must fear for mine.

OEDIPUS

For God's sake if you know of anything,
do not turn from us; all of us kneel to you,
all of us here, your suppliants.

TEIRESIAS

All of you here know nothing. I will not
bring to the light of day my troubles, mine—
rather than call them yours.

OEDIPUS

What do you mean?
You know of something but refuse to speak.
Would you betray us and destroy the city?

TEIRESIAS

I will not bring this pain upon us both,
neither on you nor on myself. Why is it
you question me and waste your labour? I
will tell you nothing.

OEDIPUS

You would provoke a stone! Tell us, you villain,
tell us, and do not stand there quietly
unmoved and balking at the final issue.

TEIRESIAS

You blame my temper but you do not see
your own that lives within you; it is me
you chide.

OEDIPUS

Who would not feel his temper rise
at words like these with which you shame our city?

TEIRESIAS

Of themselves things will come, although I hide them
and breathe no word of them.

OEDIPUS

                Since they will come
tell them to me.

TEIRESIAS

            I will say nothing further.
Against this answer let your temper rage
as wildly as you will.

OEDIPUS

             Indeed I am
so angry I shall not hold back a jot
of what I think. For I would have you know
I think you were complotter of the deed
and doer of the deed save in so far
as for the actual killing. Had you had eyes
I would have said alone you murdered him.

TEIRESIAS

Yes? Then I warn you faithfully to keep
the letter of your proclamation and
from this day forth to speak no word of greeting
to these nor me; you are the land's pollution.

OEDIPUS

How shamelessly you started up this taunt!
How do you think you will escape?

TEIRESIAS

                  I have.
I have escaped; the truth is what I cherish
and that's my strength.

OEDIPUS

            And who has taught you truth?
Not your profession surely!

TEIRESIAS

          You have taught me,
for you have made me speak against my will.

OEDIPUS

Speak what? Tell me again that I may learn it better.

TEIRESIAS

Did you not understand before or would you
provoke me into speaking?

OEDIPUS

                    I did not grasp it,
not so to call it known. Say it again.

TEIRESIAS

I say you are the murderer of the king
whose murderer you seek.

OEDIPUS

                    Not twice you shall not
say calumnies like this and stay unpunished.

TEIRESIAS

Shall I say more to tempt your anger more?

OEDIPUS

As much as you desire; it will be said
in vain.

TEIRESIAS

          I say that with those you love best
you live in foulest shame unconsciously
and do not see where you are in calamity.

OEDIPUS

Do you imagine you can always talk
like this, and live to laugh at it hereafter?

TEIRESIAS

Yes, if the truth has anything of strength.

OEDIPUS

It has, but not for you; it has no strength
for you because you are blind in mind and ears
as well as in your eyes.

TEIRESIAS

You are a poor wretch
to taunt me with the very insults which
every one soon will heap upon yourself.

OEDIPUS

Your life is one long night so that you cannot
hurt me or any other who sees the light.

TEIRESIAS

It is not fate that I should be your ruin,
Apollo is enough; it is his care
to work this out.

OEDIPUS

Was this your own design
or Creon's?

TEIRESIAS

Creon is no hurt to you,
but you are to yourself.

OEDIPUS

Wealth, sovereignty and skill outmatching skill
for the contrivance of an envied life,
great store of jealousy fill your treasury chests,
if my friend Creon, friend from the first and loyal,
thus secretly attacks me, secretly
desires to drive me out and secretly
suborns this juggling, trick devising quack,
this wily beggar who has only eyes
for his own gains, but blindness in his skill.
For, tell me, where have you seen clear, Teiresias,
with your prophetic eyes? When the dark singer,
the sphinx, was in your country, did you speak
word of deliverance to its citizens?
And yet the riddle's answer was not the province
of a chance comer. It was a prophet's task
and plainly you had no such gift of prophecy
from birds nor otherwise from any God

to glean a word of knowledge. But I came,
Oedipus, who knew nothing, and I stopped her.
I solved the riddle by my wit alone.
Mine was no knowledge got from birds. And now
you would expel me,
because you think that you will find a place
by Creon's throne. I think you will be sorry,
both you and your accomplice, for your plot
to drive me out. And did I not regard you
as an old man, some suffering would have taught you
that what was in your heart was treason.

CHORUS

We look at this man's words and yours, my king,
and we find both have spoken them in anger.
We need no angry words but only thought
how we may best hit the God's meaning for us.

TEIRESIAS

If you are king, at least I have the right
no less to speak in my defence against you.
Of that much I am master. I am no slave
of yours, but Loxias', and so I shall not
enroll myself with Creon for my patron.
Since you have taunted me with being blind,
here is my word for you.
You have your eyes but see not where you are
in sin, nor where you live, nor whom you live with.
Do you know who your parents are? Unknowing
you are an enemy to kith and kin
in death, beneath the earth, and in this life.
A deadly footed, double striking curse,
from father and mother both, shall drive you forth
out of this land, with darkness on your eyes,
that now have such straight vision. Shall there be
a place will not be harbour to your cries,
a corner of Cithaeron will not ring
in echo to your cries, soon, soon,—

when you shall learn the secret of your marriage,
which steered you to a haven in this house,—
haven no haven, after lucky voyage?
And of the multitude of other evils
establishing a grim equality
between you and your children, you know nothing.
So, muddy with contempt my words and Creon's!
there is no man shall perish as you shall.

OEDIPUS

Is it endurable that I should hear
such words from him? Go and a curse go with you!
Quick, home with you! Out of my house at once!

TEIRESIAS

I would not have come either had you not called me.

OEDIPUS

I did not know then you would talk like a fool—
or it would have been long before I called you.

TEIRESIAS

I am a fool then, as it seems to you—
but to the parents who have bred you, wise.

OEDIPUS

What parents? Stop! Who are they of all the world?

TEIRESIAS

This day will show your birth and bring your ruin.

OEDIPUS

How needlessly your riddles darken everything.

TEIRESIAS

But it's in riddle answering you are strongest.

OEDIPUS

Yes. Taunt me where you will find me great.

TEIRESIAS

It is this very luck that has destroyed you.

OEDIPUS

I do not care, if it has served this city.

TEIRESIAS

Well, I will go. Come, boy, lead me away.

OEDIPUS

Yes, lead him off. So long as you are here,
you'll be a stumbling block and a vexation;
once gone, you will not trouble me again.

TEIRESIAS

               I have said
what I came here to say not fearing your
countenance: there is no way you can hurt me.
I tell you, king, this man, this murderer
(whom you have long declared you are in search of,
indicting him in threatening proclamation
as murderer of Laius)—he is here.
In name he is a stranger among citizens
but soon he will be shown to be a citizen
true native Theban, and he'll have no joy
of the discovery: blindness for sight
and beggary for riches his exchange,
he shall go journeying to a foreign country
tapping his way before him with a stick.
He shall be proved father and brother both
to his own children in his house; to her
that gave him birth, a son and husband both;
a fellow sower in his father's bed
with that same father that he murdered.
Go within, reckon that out, and if you find me
mistaken, say I have no skill in prophecy.

        (*Exeunt separately Teiresias and Oedipus.*)

CHORUS

  Strophe

Who is the man proclaimed
by Delphi's prophetic rock

as the bloody handed murderer,
the doer of deeds that none dare name?
Now is the time for him to run
with a stronger foot
than Pegasus
for the child of Zeus leaps in arms upon him
with fire and the lightning bolt,
and terribly close on his heels
are the Fates that never miss.

Antistrophe

Lately from snowy Parnassus
clearly the voice flashed forth,
bidding each Theban track him down,
the unknown murderer.
In the savage forests he lurks and in
the caverns like
the mountain bull.
He is sad and lonely, and lonely his feet
that carry him far from the navel of earth;
but its prophecies, ever living,
flutter around his head.

Strophe

The augur has spread confusion,
terrible confusion;
I do not approve what was said
nor can I deny it.
I do not know what to say;
I am in a flutter of foreboding;
I never heard in the present
nor past of a quarrel between
the sons of Labdacus and Polybus,
that I might bring as proof
in attacking the popular fame
of Oedipus, seeking
to take vengeance for undiscovered
death in the line of Labdacus.

Antistrophe

Truly Zeus and Apollo are wise
and in human things all knowing;
but amongst men there is no
distinct judgment, between the prophet
and me—which of us is right.
One man may pass another in wisdom
but I would never agree
with those that find fault with the king
till I should see the word
proved right beyond doubt. For once
in visible form the Sphinx
came on him and all of us
saw his wisdom and in that test
he saved the city. So he will not be condemned by my mind.

(*Enter Creon.*)

CREON

Citizens, I have come because I heard
deadly words spread about me, that the king
accuses me. I cannot take that from him.
If he believes that in these present troubles
he has been wronged by me in word or deed
I do not want to live on with the burden
of such a scandal on me. The report
injures me doubly and most vitally—
for I'll be called a traitor to my city
and traitor also to my friends and you.

CHORUS

Perhaps it was a sudden gust of anger
that forced that insult from him, and no judgment.

CREON

But did he say that it was in compliance
with schemes of mine that the seer told him lies?

CHORUS

Yes, he said that, but why, I do not know.

CREON

Were his eyes straight in his head? Was his mind right
when he accused me in this fashion?

CHORUS

I do not know; I have no eyes to see
what princes do. Here comes the king himself.

(Enter Oedipus.)

OEDIPUS

You, sir, how is it you come here? Have you so much
brazen-faced daring that you venture in
my house although you are proved manifestly
the murderer of that man, and though you tried,
openly, highway robbery of my crown?
For God's sake, tell me what you saw in me,
what cowardice or what stupidity,
that made you lay a plot like this against me?
Did you imagine I should not observe
the crafty scheme that stole upon me or
seeing it, take no means to counter it?
Was it not stupid of you to make the attempt,
to try to hunt down royal power without
the people at your back or friends? For only
with the people at your back or money can
the hunt end in the capture of a crown.

CREON

Do you know what you're doing? Will you listen
to words to answer yours, and then pass judgment?

OEDIPUS

You're quick to speak, but I am slow to grasp you,
for I have found you dangerous,—and my foe.

CREON

First of all hear what I shall say to that.

OEDIPUS

At least don't tell me that you are not guilty.

CREON

If you believe you cherish something fine
in obstinacy without brains, you're wrong.

OEDIPUS

And you are wrong if you believe that one,
a criminal, will not be punished only
because he is my kinsman.

CREON

                              This is but just—
but tell me, then, of what offense I'm guilty?

OEDIPUS

Did you or did you not urge me to send
to this prophetic mumbler?

CREON

                              I did indeed,
and I shall stand by what I told you.

OEDIPUS

How long ago is it since Laius . . . .

CREON

What about Laius? I don't understand.

OEDIPUS

Vanished—died—was murdered?

CREON

                              It is long,
a long, long time to reckon.

OEDIPUS

                      Was this prophet
in the profession then?

CREON

                      He was, and honoured
as highly as he is today.

OEDIPUS
At that time did he say a word about me?

CREON
Never, at least when I was near him.

OEDIPUS
You never made a search for the dead man?

CREON
We searched, indeed, but never learned of anything.

OEDIPUS
Why did our wise old friend not say this then?

CREON
I don't know; and when I know nothing, I
usually hold my tongue.

OEDIPUS
              You know this much,
and can declare this much if you are loyal.

CREON
What is it? If I know I'll not deny it.

OEDIPUS
That he would not have said that I killed Laius
had he not met you first.

CREON
              You know yourself
whether he said this, but I demand that I
should hear as much from you as you from me.

OEDIPUS
Then hear,—I'll not be proved a murderer.

CREON
Well, then. You're married to my sister.

OEDIPUS

                              Yes,
that I am not disposed to deny.

CREON

                        You rule
this country giving her an equal share
in the government?

OEDIPUS

                  Yes, everything she wants
she has from me.

CREON

            And I, as thirdsman to you,
am rated as the equal of you two?

OEDIPUS

Yes, and it's there you've proved yourself false friend.

CREON

Not if you will reflect on it as I do.
Consider, first, if you think any one
would choose to rule and fear rather than rule
and sleep untroubled by a fear if power
were equal in both cases. I, at least,
I was not born with such a frantic yearning
to be a king—but to do what kings do.
And so it is with every one who has learned
wisdom and self-control. As it stands now,
the prizes are all mine—and without fear.
But if I were the king myself, I must
do much that went against the grain.
How should despotic rule seem sweeter to me
than painless power and an assured authority?
I am not so besotted yet that I
want other honours than those that come with profit.
Now every man's my pleasure; every man greets me;
now those who are your suitors fawn on me,—
success for them depends upon my favour.
Why should I let all this go to win that?

My mind would not be traitor if it's wise;
I am no treason lover, of my nature,
nor would I ever dare to join a plot.
Prove what I say. Go to the oracle
at Pytho and inquire about the answers,
if they are as I told you. For the rest,
if you discover I laid any plot
together with the seer, kill me, I say,
not only by your vote but by my own.
But do not charge me on obscure opinion
without some proof to back it. It's not just
lightly to count your knaves as honest men,
nor honest men as knaves. To throw away
an honest friend is, as it were, to throw
your life away, which a man loves the best.
In time you will know all with certainty;
time is the only test of honest men,
one day is space enough to know a rogue.

CHORUS

His words are wise, king, if one fears to fall.
Those who are quick of temper are not safe.

OEDIPUS

When he that plots against me secretly
moves quickly, I must quickly counterplot.
If I wait taking no decisive measure
his business will be done, and mine be spoiled.

CREON

What do you want to do then? Banish me?

OEDIPUS

No, certainly; kill you, not banish you.[1]

---

[1] Two lines omitted here owing to the confusion in the dialogue consequent on the loss of a third line. The lines as they stand in Jebb's edition (1902) are:
OED.: That you may show what manner of thing is envy.
CREON: You speak as one that will not yield or trust.
[OED. lost line.]

CREON

I do not think that you've your wits about you.

OEDIPUS

For my own interests, yes.

CREON

But for mine, too,
you should think equally.

OEDIPUS

You are a rogue.

CREON

Suppose you do not understand?

OEDIPUS

But yet
I must be ruler.

CREON

Not if you rule badly.

OEDIPUS

O, city, city!

CREON

I too have some share
in the city; it is not yours alone.

CHORUS

Stop, my lords! Here—and in the nick of time
I see Jocasta coming from the house;
with her help lay the quarrel that now stirs you.

(*Enter Jocasta.*)

JOCASTA

For shame! Why have you raised this foolish squabbling
brawl? Are you not ashamed to air your private
griefs when the country's sick? Go in, you, Oedipus,
and you, too, Creon, into the house. Don't magnify
your nothing troubles.

CREON

                Sister, Oedipus,
your husband, thinks he has the right to do
terrible wrongs—he has but to choose between
two terrors: banishing or killing me.

OEDIPUS

He's right, Jocasta; for I find him plotting
with knavish tricks against my person.

CREON

That God may never bless me! May I die
accursed, if I have been guilty of
one tittle of the charge you bring against me!

JOCASTA

I beg you, Oedipus, trust him in this,
spare him for the sake of this his oath to God,
for my sake, and the sake of those who stand here.

CHORUS

Be gracious, be merciful,
we beg of you.

OEDIPUS

In what would you have me yield?

CHORUS

He has been no silly child in the past.
He is strong in his oath now.
Spare him.

OEDIPUS

Do you know what you ask?

CHORUS

Yes.

OEDIPUS

Tell me then.

CHORUS

He has been your friend before all men's eyes; do not cast him away dishonoured on an obscure conjecture.

OEDIPUS

I would have you know that this request of yours
really requests my death or banishment.

CHORUS

May the Sun God, king of Gods, forbid! May I die without God's blessing, without friends' help, if I had any such thought. But my spirit is broken by my unhappiness for my wasting country; and this would but add troubles amongst ourselves to the other troubles.

OEDIPUS

Well, let him go then—if I must die ten times for it,
or be sent out dishonoured into exile.
It is your lips that prayed for him I pitied,
not his; wherever he is, I shall hate him.

CREON

I see you sulk in yielding and you're dangerous
when you are out of temper; natures like yours
are justly heaviest for themselves to bear.

OEDIPUS

Leave me alone! Take yourself off, I tell you.

CREON

I'll go, you have not known me, but they have,
and they have known my innocence.

(*Exit.*)

CHORUS

Won't you take him inside, lady?

JOCASTA

Yes, when I've found out what was the matter.

CHORUS

There was some misconceived suspicion of a story, and on
the other side the sting of injustice.

JOCASTA

So, on both sides?

CHORUS

Yes.

JOCASTA

What was the story?

CHORUS

I think it best, in the interests of the country, to leave it
where it ended.

OEDIPUS

You see where you have ended, straight of judgment
although you are, by softening my anger.

CHORUS

Sir, I have said before and I say again—be sure that I would
have been proved a madman, bankrupt in sane council, if I
should put you away, you who steered the country I love
safely when she was crazed with troubles. God grant that
now, too, you may prove a fortunate guide for us.

JOCASTA

Tell me, my lord, I beg of you, what was it
that roused your anger so?

OEDIPUS

                    Yes, I will tell you.
I honour you more than I honour them.
It was Creon and the plots he laid against me.

JOCASTA

Tell me—if you can clearly tell the quarrel—

OEDIPUS

                             Creon says
that I'm the murderer of Laius.

JOCASTA

Of his own knowledge or on information?

OEDIPUS

He sent this rascal prophet to me, since
he keeps his own mouth clean of any guilt.

JOCASTA

Do not concern yourself about this matter;
listen to me and learn that human beings
have no part in the craft of prophecy.
Of that I'll show you a short proof.
There was an oracle once that came to Laius,—
I will not say that it was Phoebus' own,
but it was from his servants—and it told him
that it was fate that he should die a victim
at the hands of his own son, a son to be born
of Laius and me. But, see now, he,
the king, was killed by foreign highway robbers
at a place where three roads meet—so goes the story;
and for the son—before three days were out
after his birth King Laius pierced his ankles
and by the hands of others cast him forth
upon a pathless hillside. So Apollo
failed to fulfill his oracle to the son,
that he should kill his father, and to Laius
also proved false in that the thing he feared,
death at his son's hands, never came to pass.
So clear in this case were the oracles,
so clear and false. Give them no heed, I say;
what God discovers need of, easily
he shows to us himself.

OEDIPUS
                    O dear Jocasta,
as I hear this from you, there comes upon me
a wandering of the soul—I could run mad.

JOCASTA
What trouble is it, that you turn again
and speak like this?

OEDIPUS
                    I thought I heard you say
that Laius was killed at a crossroads.

JOCASTA
Yes, that was how the story went and still
that word goes round.

OEDIPUS
                    Where is this place, Jocasta,
where he was murdered?

JOCASTA
                    Phocis is the country
and the road splits there, one of two roads from Delphi,
another comes from Daulia.

OEDIPUS
                    How long ago is this?
JOCASTA
The news came to the city just before
you became king and all men's eyes looked to you.
What is it, Oedipus, that's in your mind?

OEDIPUS
Don't ask me yet—tell me of Laius—
how did he look? How old or young was he?

JOCASTA
He was a tall man and his hair was grizzled
already—nearly white—and in his form
not unlike you.

OEDIPUS

     O God, I think I have
called curses on myself in ignorance.

JOCASTA

What do you mean? I am terrified
when I look at you.

OEDIPUS

     I have a deadly fear
that the old seer had eyes. You'll show me more
if you can tell me one more thing.

JOCASTA

        I will.
I'm frightened,—but if I can understand,
I'll tell you all you ask.

OEDIPUS

     How was his company?
Had he few with him when he went this journey,
or many servants, as would suit a prince?

JOCASTA

In all there were but five, and among them
a herald; and one carriage for the king.

OEDIPUS

It's plain—it's plain—who was it told you this?

JOCASTA

The only servant that escaped safe home.

OEDIPUS

Is he at home now?

JOCASTA

     No, when he came home again
and saw you king and Laius was dead,
he came to me and touched my hand and begged
that I should send him to the fields to be

my shepherd and so he might see the city
as far off as he might. So I
sent him away. He was an honest man,
as slaves go, and was worthy of far more
than what he asked of me.

OEDIPUS

O, how I wish that he could come back quickly!

JOCASTA

He can. Why is your heart so set on this?

OEDIPUS

O dear Jocasta, I am full of fears
that I have spoken far too much; and therefore
I wish to see this shepherd.

JOCASTA

                       He will come;
but, Oedipus, I think I'm worthy too
to know what is it that disquiets you.

OEDIPUS

It shall not be kept from you, since my mind
has gone so far with its forebodings. Whom
should I confide in rather than you, who is there
of more importance to me who have passed
through such a fortune?
Polybus was my father, king of Corinth,
and Merope, the Dorian, my mother.
I was held greatest of the citizens
in Corinth till a curious chance befell me
as I shall tell you—curious, indeed,
but hardly worth the store I set upon it.
There was a dinner and at it a man,
a drunken man, accused me in his drink
of being bastard. I was furious
but held my temper under for that day.

Next day I went and taxed my parents with it;
they took the insult very ill from him,
the drunken fellow who had uttered it.
So I was comforted for their part, but
still this thing rankled always, for the story
crept about widely. And I went at last
to Pytho, though my parents did not know.
But Phoebus sent me home again unhonoured
in what I came to learn, but he foretold
other and desperate horrors to befall me,
that I was fated to lie with my mother,
and show to daylight an accursed breed
which men would not endure, and I was doomed
to be murderer of the father that begot me.
When I heard this I fled, and in the days
that followed I would measure from the stars
the whereabouts of Corinth—yes, I fled
to somewhere where I should not see fulfilled
the infamies told in that dreadful oracle.
And as I journeyed I came to the place
where, as you say, this king met with his death.
Jocasta, I will tell you the whole truth.
When I was near the branching of the crossroads,
going on foot, I was encountered by
a herald and a carriage with a man in it,
just as you tell me. He that led the way
and the old man himself wanted to thrust me
out of the road by force. I became angry
and struck the coachman who was pushing me.
When the old man saw this he watched his moment,
and as I passed he struck me from his carriage,
full on the head with his two pointed goad.
But he was paid in full and presently
my stick had struck him backwards from the car
and he rolled out of it. And then I killed them
all. If it happened there was any tie
of kinship twixt this man and Laius,
who is then now more miserable than I,

what man on earth so hated by the Gods,
since neither citizen nor foreigner
may welcome me at home or even greet me,
but drive me out of doors? And it is I,
I and no other have so cursed myself.
And I pollute the bed of him I killed
by the hands that killed him. Was I not born evil?
Am I not utterly unclean? I had to fly
and in my banishment not even see
my kindred nor set foot in my own country,
or otherwise my fate was to be yoked
in marriage with my mother and kill my father,
Polybus who begot me and had reared me.
Would not one rightly judge and say that on me
these things were sent by some malignant God?
O no, no, no—O holy majesty
of God on high, may I not see that day!
May I be gone out of men's sight before
I see the deadly taint of this disaster
come upon me.

CHORUS

Sir, we too fear these things. But until you see this man face
to face and hear his story, hope.

OEDIPUS

Yes, I have just this much of hope—to wait until the herdsman comes.

JOCASTA

And when he comes, what do you want with him?

OEDIPUS

I'll tell you; if I find that his story is the same as yours, I at
least will be clear of this guilt.

JOCASTA

Why what so particularly did you learn from my story?

OEDIPUS

You said that he spoke of highway *robbers* who killed Laius.
Now if he uses the same number, it was not I who killed him.
One man cannot be the same as many. But if he speaks of a
man travelling alone, then clearly the burden of the guilt
inclines towards me.

JOCASTA

Be sure, at least, that this was how he told the story. He cannot unsay it now, for every one in the city heard it—not I
alone. But, Oedipus, even if he diverges from what he said
then, he shall never prove that the murder of Laius squares
rightly with the prophecy—for Loxias declared that the king
should be killed by his own son. And that poor creature did
not kill him surely,—for he died himself first. So as far as
prophecy goes, henceforward I shall not look to the right
hand or the left.

OEDIPUS

Right. But yet, send some one for the peasant to bring him
here; do not neglect it.

JOCASTA

I will send quickly. Now let me go indoors. I will do nothing except what pleases you.

(*Exeunt.*)

CHORUS

Strophe

May destiny ever find me
pious in word and deed
prescribed by the laws that live on high:
laws begotten in the clear air of heaven,
whose only father is Olympus;
no mortal nature brought them to birth,
no forgetfulness shall lull them to sleep;
for God is great in them and grows not old.

Antistrophe

Insolence breeds the tyrant, insolence
if it is glutted with a surfeit, unseasonable, unprofitable,
climbs to the roof-top and plunges
sheer down to the ruin that must be,
and there its feet are no service.
But I pray that the God may never
abolish the eager ambition that profits the state.
For I shall never cease to hold the God as our protector.

Strophe

If a man walks with haughtiness
of hand or word and gives no heed
to Justice and the shrines of Gods
despises—may an evil doom
smite him for his ill-starred pride of heart!—
if he reaps gains without justice
and will not hold from impiety
and his fingers itch for untouchable things.
When such things are done, what man shall contrive
to shield his soul from the shafts of the God?
When such deeds are held in honour,
why should I honour the Gods in the dance?

Antistrophe

No longer to the holy place,
to the navel of earth I'll go
to worship, nor to Abae
nor to Olympia,
unless the oracles are proved to fit,
for all men's hands to point at.
O Zeus, if you are rightly called
the sovereign lord, all-mastering,
let this not escape you nor your ever-living power!
The oracles concerning Laius
are old and dim and men regard them not.
Apollo is nowhere clear in honour; God's service perishes.

(Enter Jocasta, carrying garlands.)

JOCASTA

Princes of the land, I have had the thought to go
to the Gods' temples, bringing in my hand
garlands and gifts of incense, as you see.
For Oedipus excites himself too much
at every sort of trouble, not conjecturing,
like a man of sense, what will be from what was,
but he is always at the speaker's mercy,
when he speaks terrors. I can do no good
by my advice, and so I came as suppliant
to you, Lycaean Apollo, who are nearest.
These are the symbols of my prayer and this
my prayer: grant us escape free of the curse.
Now when we look to him we are all afraid;
he's pilot of our ship and he is frightened.

(Enter a Messenger.)

MESSENGER

Might I learn from you, sirs, where is the house of Oedipus?
Or best of all, if you know, where is the king himself?

CHORUS

This is his house and he is within doors. This lady is his wife
and mother of his children.

MESSENGER

God bless you, lady, and God bless your household! God
bless Oedipus' noble wife!

JOCASTA

God bless you, sir, for your kind greeting! What do you
want of us that you have come here? What have you to tell
us?

MESSENGER

Good news, lady. Good for your house and for your husband.

JOCASTA

What is your news? Who sent you to us?

MESSENGER

I come from Corinth and the news I bring will give you pleasure. Perhaps a little pain too.

JOCASTA

What is this news of double meaning?

MESSENGER

The people of the Isthmus will choose Oedipus to be their king. That is the rumour there.

JOCASTA

But isn't their king still old Polybus?

MESSENGER

No. He is in his grave. Death has got him.

JOCASTA

Is that the truth? Is Oedipus' father dead?

MESSENGER

May I die myself if it be otherwise!

JOCASTA (*to a servant*)

Be quick and run to the King with the news! O oracles of the Gods, where are you now? It was from this man Oedipus fled, lest he should be his murderer! And now he is dead, in the course of nature, and not killed by Oedipus.

(*Enter Oedipus.*)

OEDIPUS

Dearest Jocasta, why have you sent for me?

JOCASTA

Listen to this man and when you hear reflect what is the outcome of the holy oracles of the Gods.

OEDIPUS

Who is he? What is his message for me?

JOCASTA

He is from Corinth and he tells us that your father Polybus
is dead and gone.

OEDIPUS

What's this you say, sir? Tell me yourself.

MESSENGER

Since this is the first matter you want clearly told: Polybus
has gone down to death. You may be sure of it.

OEDIPUS

By treachery or sickness?

MESSENGER

A small thing will put old bodies asleep.

OEDIPUS

So he died of sickness, it seems,—poor old man!

MESSENGER

Yes, and of age—the long years he had measured.

OEDIPUS

Ha! Ha! O dear Jocasta, why should one
look to the Pythian hearth? Why should one look
to the birds screaming overhead? They prophesied
that I should kill my father! But he's dead,
and hidden deep in earth, and I stand here
who never laid a hand on spear against him,—
unless perhaps he died of longing for me,
and thus I am his murderer. But they,
the oracles, as they stand—he's taken them
away with him, they're dead as he himself is,
and worthless.

JOCASTA
> That I told you before now.

OEDIPUS
You did, but I was misled by my fear.

JOCASTA
Then lay no more of them to heart, not one.

OEDIPUS
But surely I must fear my mother's bed?

JOCASTA
Why should man fear since chance is all in all
for him, and he can clearly foreknow nothing?
Best to live lightly, as one can, unthinkingly.
As to your mother's marriage bed,—don't fear it.
Before this, in dreams too, as well as oracles,
many a man has lain with his own mother.
But he to whom such things are nothing bears
his life most easily.

OEDIPUS
All that you say would be said perfectly
if she were dead; but since she lives I must
still fear, although you talk so well, Jocasta.

JOCASTA
Still in your father's death there's light of comfort?

OEDIPUS
Great light of comfort; but I fear the living.

MESSENGER
Who is the woman that makes you afraid?

OEDIPUS
Merope, old man, Polybus' wife.

MESSENGER
What about her frightens the queen and you?

OEDIPUS

A terrible oracle, stranger, from the Gods.

MESSENGER

Can it be told? Or does the sacred law
forbid another to have knowledge of it?

OEDIPUS

O no! Once on a time Loxias said
that I should lie with my own mother and
take on my hands the blood of my own father.
And so for these long years I've lived away
from Corinth; it has been to my great happiness;
but yet it's sweet to see the face of parents.

MESSENGER

This was the fear which drove you out of Corinth?

OEDIPUS

Old man, I did not wish to kill my father.

MESSENGER

Why should I not free you from this fear, sir,
since I have come to you in all goodwill?

OEDIPUS

You would not find me thankless if you did.

MESSENGER

Why, it was just for this I brought the news,—
to earn your thanks when you had come safe home.

OEDIPUS

No, I will never come near my parents.

MESSENGER

                              Son,
it's very plain you don't know what you're doing.

OEDIPUS
What do you mean, old man? For God's sake, tell me.

MESSENGER
If your homecoming is checked by fears like these.

OEDIPUS
Yes, I'm afraid that Phoebus may prove right.

MESSENGER
The murder and the incest?

OEDIPUS
                              Yes, old man;
that is my constant terror.

MESSENGER
                    Do you know
that all your fears are empty?

OEDIPUS
                        How is that,
if they are father and mother and I their son?

MESSENGER
Because Polybus was no kin to you in blood.

OEDIPUS
What, was not Polybus my father?

MESSENGER
No more than I but just so much.

OEDIPUS
                              How can
my father be my father as much as one
that's nothing to me?

MESSENGER
                  Neither he nor I
begat you.

OEDIPUS
        Why then did he call me son?

MESSENGER
A gift he took you from these hands of mine.

OEDIPUS
Did he love so much what he took from another's hand?

MESSENGER
His childlessness before persuaded him.

OEDIPUS
Was I a child you bought or found when I
was given to him?

MESSENGER
        On Cithaeron's slopes
in the twisting thickets you were found.

OEDIPUS
                And why
were you a traveller in those parts?

MESSENGER
                I was
in charge of mountain flocks.

OEDIPUS
        You were a shepherd?
A hireling vagrant?

MESSENGER
        Yes, but at least at that time
the man that saved your life, son.

OEDIPUS
What ailed me when you took me in your arms?

MESSENGER
In that your ankles should be witnesses.

OEDIPUS
Why do you speak of that old pain?

MESSENGER
                    I loosed you;
the tendons of your feet were pierced and fettered,—

OEDIPUS
My swaddling clothes brought me a rare disgrace.

MESSENGER
So that from this you're called your present name.

OEDIPUS
Was this my father's doing or my mother's?
For God's sake, tell me.

MESSENGER
                    I don't know, but he
who gave you to me has more knowledge than I.

OEDIPUS
You yourself did not find me then? You took me
from someone else?

MESSENGER
                    Yes, from another shepherd.
OEDIPUS
Who was he? Do you know him well enough
to tell?

MESSENGER
          He was called Laius' man.

OEDIPUS
You mean the king who reigned here in the old days?

MESSENGER
Yes, he was that man's shepherd.

OEDIPUS
                                    Is he alive
still, so that I could see him?

MESSENGER
                            You who live here
would know that best.

OEDIPUS
                            Do any of you here
know of this shepherd whom he speaks about
in town or in the fields? Tell me. It's time
that this was found out once for all.

CHORUS
I think he is none other than the peasant
whom you have sought to see already; but
Jocasta here can tell us best of that.

OEDIPUS
Jocasta, do you know about this man
whom we have sent for? Is he the man he mentions?

JOCASTA
Why ask of whom he spoke? Don't give it heed;
nor try to keep in mind what has been said.
It will be wasted labour.

OEDIPUS
                            With such clues
I could not fail to bring my birth to light.

JOCASTA
I beg you—do not hunt this out—I beg you,
if you have any care for your own life.
What I am suffering is enough.

OEDIPUS
                            Keep up
your heart, Jocasta. Though I'm proved a slave,
thrice slave, and though my mother is thrice slave,
you'll not be shown to be of lowly lineage.

JOCASTA

O be persuaded by me, I entreat you;
do not do this.

OEDIPUS

I will not be persuaded to let be
the chance of finding out the whole thing clearly.

JOCASTA

It is because I wish you well that I
give you this counsel—and it's the best counsel.

OEDIPUS

Then the best counsel vexes me, and has
for some while since.

JOCASTA

　　　　　O Oedipus, God help you!
God keep you from the knowledge of who you are!

OEDIPUS

Here, some one, go and fetch the shepherd for me;
and let her find her joy in her rich family!

JOCASTA

O Oedipus, unhappy Oedipus!
that is all I can call you, and the last thing
that I shall ever call you.

　　　　　　　　(*Exit.*)

CHORUS

Why has the queen gone, Oedipus, in wild
grief rushing from us? I am afraid that trouble
will break out of this silence.

OEDIPUS

Break out what will! I at least shall be
willing to see my ancestry, though humble.
Perhaps she is ashamed of my low birth,

for she has all a woman's high-flown pride.
But I account myself a child of Fortune,
beneficent Fortune, and I shall not be
dishonoured. She's the mother from whom I spring;
the months, my brothers, marked me, now as small,
and now again as mighty. Such is my breeding,
and I shall never prove so false to it,
as not to find the secret of my birth.

CHORUS

Strophe

If I am a prophet and wise of heart
you shall not fail, Cithaeron,
by the limitless sky, you shall not!—
to know at tomorrow's full moon
that Oedipus honours you,
as native to him and mother and nurse at once;
and that you are honoured in dancing by us, as finding
    favour in sight of our king.
Apollo, to whom we cry, find these things pleasing!

Antistrophe

Who was it bore you, child? One of
the long-lived nymphs who lay with Pan—
the father who treads the hills?
Or was she a bride of Loxias, your mother? The grassy
    slopes
are all of them dear to him. Or perhaps Cyllene's king
or the Bacchants' God that lives on the tops
of the hills received you a gift from some
one of the Helicon Nymphs, with whom he mostly plays?

(*Enter an old man, led by Oedipus' servants.*)

OEDIPUS

If some one like myself who never met him
may make a guess,—I think this is the herdsman,
whom we were seeking. His old age is consonant
with the other. And besides, the men who bring him
I recognize as my own servants. You

perhaps may better me in knowledge since
you've seen the man before.

CHORUS

You can be sure
I recognize him. For if Laius
had ever an honest shepherd, this was he.

OEDIPUS

You, sir, from Corinth, I must ask you first,
is this the man you spoke of?

MESSENGER

This is he
before your eyes.

OEDIPUS

Old man, look here at me
and tell me what I ask you. Were you ever
a servant of King Laius?

HERDSMAN

I was,—
no slave he bought but reared in his own house.

OEDIPUS

What did you do as work? How did you live?

HERDSMAN

Most of my life was spent among the flocks.

OEDIPUS

In what part of the country did you live?

HERDSMAN

Cithaeron and the places near to it.

OEDIPUS

And somewhere there perhaps you knew this man?

HERDSMAN

What was his occupation? Who?

OEDIPUS

                        This man here,
have you had any dealings with him?

HERDSMAN

                        No—
not such that I can quickly call to mind.

MESSENGER

That is no wonder, master. But I'll make him remember
what he does not know. For I know, that he well knows the
country of Cithaeron, how he with two flocks, I with one
kept company for three years—each year half a year—from
spring till autumn time and then when winter came I drove
my flocks to our fold home again and he to Laius' steadings.
Well—am I right or not in what I said we did?

HERDSMAN

You're right—although it's a long time ago.

MESSENGER

Do you remember giving me a child
to bring up as my foster child?

HERDSMAN

                        What's this?
Why do you ask this question?

MESSENGER

                        Look, old man,
here he is—here's the man who was that child!

HERDSMAN

Death take you! Won't you hold your tongue?

OEDIPUS

                        No, no,
do not find fault with him, old man. Your words
are more at fault than his.

HERDSMAN
                        O best of masters,
how do I give offense?

OEDIPUS
                        When you refuse
to speak about the child of whom he asks you.

HERDSMAN
He speaks out of his ignorance, without meaning.

OEDIPUS
If you'll not talk to gratify me, you
will talk with pain to urge you.

HERDSMAN
                        O please, sir,
don't hurt an old man, sir.

OEDIPUS (*to the servants*)
                        Here, one of you,
twist his hands behind him.

HERDSMAN
            Why, God help me, why?
What do you want to know?

OEDIPUS
                        You gave a child
to him,—the child he asked you of?

HERDSMAN
                        I did.
I wish I'd died the day I did.

OEDIPUS
                        You will
unless you tell me truly.

HERDSMAN
                  And I'll die
far worse if I should tell you.

OEDIPUS
                              This fellow
is bent on more delays, as it would seem.

HERDSMAN

O no, no! I have told you that I gave it.

OEDIPUS

Where did you get this child from? Was it your own
or did you get it from another?

HERDSMAN
                                        Not
my own at all; I had it from some one.

OEDIPUS

One of these citizens? or from what house?

HERDSMAN

O master, please—I beg you, master, please
don't ask me more.

OEDIPUS
                    You're a dead man if I
ask you again.

HERDSMAN
                    It was one of the children
of Laius.

OEDIPUS
            A slave? Or born in wedlock?
HERDSMAN

O God, I am on the brink of frightful speech.

OEDIPUS

And I of frightful hearing. But I must hear.

HERDSMAN

The child was called his child; but she within,
your wife would tell you best how all this was.

OEDIPUS
She gave it to you?

HERDSMAN
                    Yes, she did, my lord.
OEDIPUS
To do what with it?

HERDSMAN
                    Make away with it.
OEDIPUS
She was so hard—its mother?

HERDSMAN
                         Aye, through fear
of evil oracles.

OEDIPUS
                         Which?

HERDSMAN
                    They said that he
should kill his parents.

OEDIPUS
                    How was it that you
gave it away to this old man?

HERDSMAN
                              O master,
I pitied it, and thought that I could send it
off to another country and this man
was from another country. But he saved it
for the most terrible troubles. If you are
the man he says you are, you're bred to misery.

OEDIPUS
O, O, O, they will all come,
all come out clearly! Light of the sun, let me
look upon you no more after today!

I who first saw the light bred of a match
accursed, and accursed in my living
with them I lived with, cursed in my killing.

(Exeunt all but the Chorus.)

CHORUS

Strophe

O generations of men, how I
count you as equal with those who live
not at all!
what man, what man on earth wins more
of happiness than a seeming
and after that turning away?

Oedipus, you are my pattern of this,
Oedipus, you and your fate!
Luckless Oedipus, whom of all men
I envy not at all.

Antistrophe

In as much as he shot his bolt
beyond the others and won the prize
of happiness complete—
O Zeus—and killed and reduced to nought
the hooked taloned maid of the riddling speech,
standing a tower against death for my land:
hence he was called my king and hence
was honoured the highest of all
honours; and hence he ruled
in the great city of Thebes.

Strophe

But now whose tale is more miserable?
Who is there lives with a savager fate?
Whose troubles so reverse his life as his?

O Oedipus, the famous prince
for whom a great haven
the same both as father and son

sufficed for generation,
how, O how, have the furrows ploughed
by your father endured to bear you, poor wretch,
and hold their peace so long?

Antistrophe

Time who sees all has found you out
against your will; judges your marriage accursed,
begetter and begot at one in it.

O child of Laius,
would I had never seen you,
I weep for you and cry
a dirge of lamentation.

To speak directly, I drew my breath
from you at the first and so now I lull
my mouth to sleep with your name.

(*Enter a second messenger.*)

SECOND MESSENGER

O Princes always honoured by our country,
what deeds you'll hear of and what horrors see
what grief you'll feel, if you as true born Thebans
care for the house of Labdacus's sons.
Phasis nor Ister cannot purge this house,
I think, with all their streams, such things
it hides, such evils shortly will bring forth
into the light, whether they will or not;
and troubles hurt the most
when they prove self-inflicted.

CHORUS

What we had known before did not fall short
of bitter groaning's worth; what's more to tell?

SECOND MESSENGER

Shortest to hear and tell—our glorious queen
Jocasta's dead.

CHORUS

                   Unhappy woman! How?

SECOND MESSENGER

By her own hand. The worst of what was done
you cannot know. You did not see the sight.
Yet in so far as I remember it
you'll hear the end of our unlucky queen.
When she came raging into the house she went
straight to her marriage bed, tearing her hair
with both her hands, and crying upon Laius
long dead—Do you remember, Laius,
that night long past which bred a child for us
to send you to your death and leave
a mother making children with her son?
And then she groaned and cursed the bed in which
she brought forth husband by her husband, children
by her own child, an infamous double bond.
How after that she died I do not know,—
for Oedipus distracted us from seeing.
He burst upon us shouting and we looked
to him as he paced frantically around,
begging us always: Give me a sword, I say,
to find this wife no wife, this mother's womb,
this field of double sowing whence I sprang
and where I sowed my children! As he raved
some god showed him the way—none of us there.
Bellowing terribly and led by some
invisible guide he rushed on the two doors,—
wrenching the hollow bolts out of their sockets,
he charged inside. There, there, we saw his wife
hanging, the twisted rope around her neck.
When he saw her, he cried out fearfully
and cut the dangling noose. Then, as she lay,
poor woman, on the ground, what happened after,
was terrible to see. He tore the brooches—
the gold chased brooches fastening her robe—
away from her and lifting them up high
dashed them on his own eyeballs, shrieking out

such things as: they will never see the crime
I have committed or had done upon me!
Dark eyes, now in the days to come look on
forbidden faces, do not recognize
those whom you long for—with such imprecations
he struck his eyes again and yet again
with the brooches. And the bleeding eyeballs gushed
and stained his beard—no sluggish oozing drops
but a black rain and bloody hail poured down.

So it has broken—and not on one head
but troubles mixed for husband and for wife.
The fortune of the days gone by was true
good fortune—but today groans and destruction
and death and shame—of all ills can be named
not one is missing.

CHORUS

Is he now in any ease from pain?

SECOND MESSENGER

                       He shouts
for some one to unbar the doors and show him
to all the men of Thebes, his father's killer,
his mother's—no I cannot say the word,
it is unholy—for he'll cast himself,
out of the land, he says, and not remain
to bring a curse upon his house, the curse
he called upon it in his proclamation. But
he wants for strength, aye, and some one to guide him;
his sickness is too great to bear. You, too,
will be shown that. The bolts are opening.
Soon you will see a sight to waken pity
even in the horror of it.

(Enter the blinded Oedipus.)

CHORUS

This is a terrible sight for men to see!
I never found a worse!
Poor wretch, what madness came upon you!

What evil spirit leaped upon your life
to your ill-luck—a leap beyond man's strength!
Indeed I pity you, but I cannot
look at you, though there's much I want to ask
and much to learn and much to see.
I shudder at the sight of you.

OEDIPUS

O, O,
where am I going? Where is my voice
borne on the wind to and fro?
Spirit, how far have you sprung?

CHORUS

To a terrible place whereof men's ears
may not hear, nor their eyes behold it.

OEDIPUS

Darkness!
Horror of darkness enfolding, resistless, unspeakable
    visitant sped by an ill wind in haste!
madness and stabbing pain and memory
of evil deeds I have done!

CHORUS

In such misfortunes it's no wonder
if double weighs the burden of your grief.

OEDIPUS

My friend,
you are the only one steadfast, the only one that
    attends on me;
you still stay nursing the blind man.
Your care is not unnoticed. I can know
your voice, although this darkness is my world.

CHORUS

Doer of dreadful deeds, how did you dare
so far to do despite to your own eyes?
what spirit urged you to it?

OEDIPUS

It was Apollo, friends, Apollo,
that brought this bitter bitterness, my sorrows to comple-
    tion.
But the hand that struck me
was none but my own.
Why should I see
whose vision showed me nothing sweet to see?

CHORUS

These things are as you say.

OEDIPUS

What can I see to love?
What greeting can touch my ears with joy?
Take me away, and haste—to a place out of the way!
Take me away, my friends, the greatly miserable,
the most accursed, whom God too hates
above all men on earth!

CHORUS

Unhappy in your mind and your misfortune,
would I had never known you!

OEDIPUS

Curse on the man who took
the cruel bonds from off my legs, as I lay in the field.
He stole me from death and saved me,
no kindly service.
Had I died then
I would not be so burdensome to friends.

CHORUS

I, too, could have wished it had been so.

OEDIPUS

Then I would not have come
to kill my father and marry my mother infamously.
Now I am godless and child of impurity,

begetter in the same seed that created my wretched self.
If there is any ill worse than ill,
that is the lot of Oedipus.

CHORUS

I cannot say your remedy was good;
you would be better dead than blind and living.

OEDIPUS

What I have done here was best done—don't tell me
otherwise, do not give me further counsel.
I do not know with what eyes I could look
upon my father when I die and go
under the earth, nor yet my wretched mother—
those two to whom I have done things deserving
worse punishment than hanging. Would the sight
of children, bred as mine are, gladden me?
No, not these eyes, never. And my city,
its towers and sacred places of the Gods,
of these I robbed my miserable self
when I commanded all to drive *him* out,
the criminal since proved by God impure
and of the race of Laius.
To this guilt I bore witness against myself—
with what eyes shall I look upon my people?
No. If there were a means to choke the fountain
of hearing I would not have stayed my hand
from locking up my miserable carcase,
seeing and hearing nothing; it is sweet
to keep our thoughts out of the range of hurt.

Cithaeron, why did you receive me? why
having received me did you not kill me straight?
And so I had not shown to men my birth.

O Polybus and Corinth and the house,
the old house that I used to call my father's—
what fairness you were nurse to, and what foulness
festered beneath! Now I am found to be

a sinner and a son of sinners. Crossroads,
and hidden glade, oak and the narrow way
at the crossroads, that drank my father's blood
offered you by my hands, do you remember
still what I did as you looked on, and what
I did when I came here? O marriage, marriage!
you bred me and again when you had bred
bred children of your child and showed to men
brides, wives and mothers and the foulest deeds
that can be in this world of ours.

Come—it's unfit to say what is unfit
to do.—I beg of you in God's name hide me
somewhere outside your country, yes, or kill me,
or throw me into the sea, to be forever
out of your sight. Approach and deign to touch me
for all my wretchedness, and do not fear.
No man but I can bear my evil doom.

CHORUS

Here Creon comes in fit time to perform
or give advice in what you ask of us.
Creon is left sole ruler in your stead.

OEDIPUS

Creon! Creon! What shall I say to him?
How can I justly hope that he will trust me?
In what is past I have been proved towards him
an utter liar.

(Enter Creon.)

CREON

Oedipus, I've come
not so that I might laugh at you nor taunt you
with evil of the past. But if you still
are without shame before the face of men
reverence at least the flame that gives all life,
our Lord the Sun, and do not show unveiled
to him pollution such that neither land
nor holy rain nor light of day can welcome.

(To a servant.)

Be quick and take him in. It is most decent
that only kin should see and hear the troubles
of kin.

OEDIPUS

       I beg you, since you've torn me from
my dreadful expectations and have come
in a most noble spirit to a man
that has used you vilely—do a thing for me.
I shall speak for your own good, not for my own.

CREON

What do you need that you would ask of me?

OEDIPUS

Drive me from here with all the speed you can
to where I may not hear a human voice.

CREON

Be sure, I would have done this had not I
wished first of all to learn from the God the course
of action I should follow.

OEDIPUS

           But his word
has been quite clear to let the parricide,
the sinner, die.

CREON

          Yes, that indeed was said.
But in the present need we had best discover
what we should do.

OEDIPUS

           And will you ask about
a man so wretched?

CREON

          Now even you will trust
the God.

Oedipus

 So. I command you—and will beseech you—
to her that lies inside that house give burial
as you would have it; she is yours and rightly
you will perform the rites for her. For me—
never let this my father's city have me
living a dweller in it. Leave me live
in the mountains where Cithaeron is, that's called
my mountain, which my mother and my father
while they were living would have made my tomb.
So I may die by their decree who sought
indeed to kill me. Yet I know this much:
no sickness and no other thing will kill me.
I would not have been saved from death if not
for some strange evil fate. Well, let my fate
go where it will.
     Creon, you need not care
about my sons; they're men and so wherever
they are, they will not lack a livelihood.
But my two girls—so sad and pitiful—
whose table never stood apart from mine,
and everything I touched they always shared—
O Creon, have a thought for them! And most
I wish that you might suffer me to touch them
and sorrow with them.

 (*Enter Antigone and Ismene, Oedipus' two daughters.*)
O my lord! O true noble Creon! Can I
really be touching them, as when I saw?
What shall I say?
Yes, I can hear them sobbing—my two darlings!
and Creon has had pity and has sent me
what I loved most?
Am I right?

Creon

You're right: it was I gave you this
because I knew from old days how you loved them
as I see now.

OEDIPUS

    God bless you for it, Creon,
and may God guard you better on your road
than he did me!

      O children,
where are you? Come here, come to my hands,
a brother's hands which turned your father's eyes,
those bright eyes you knew once, to what you see,
a father seeing nothing, knowing nothing,
begetting you from his own source of life.
I weep for you—I cannot see your faces—
I weep when I think of the bitterness
there will be in your lives, how you must live
before the world. At what assemblages
of citizens will you make one? to what
gay company will you go and not come home
in tears instead of sharing in the holiday?
And when you're ripe for marriage, who will he be,
the man who'll risk to take such infamy
as shall cling to my children, to bring hurt
on them and those that marry with them? What
curse is not there? "Your father killed his father
and sowed the seed where he had sprung himself
and begot you out of the womb that held him."
These insults you will hear. Then who will marry you?
No one, my children; clearly you are doomed
to waste away in barrenness unmarried.
Son of Menoeceus, since you are all the father
left these two girls, and we, their parents, both
are dead to them—do not allow them wander
like beggars, poor and husbandless.
They are of your own blood.
And do not make them equal with myself
in wretchedness; for you can see them now
so young, so utterly alone, save for you only.
Touch my hand, noble Creon, and say yes.
If you were older, children, and were wiser,
there's much advice I'd give you. But as it is,

let this be what you pray: give me a life
wherever there is opportunity
to live, and better life than was my father's.

CREON

Your tears have had enough of scope; now go within the
house.

OEDIPUS

I must obey, though bitter of heart.

CREON

In season, all is good.

OEDIPUS

Do you know on what conditions I obey?

CREON

You tell me them,
and I shall know them when I hear.

OEDIPUS

That you shall send me out
to live away from Thebes.

CREON

That gift you must ask of the God.

OEDIPUS

But I'm now hated by the Gods.

CREON

So quickly you'll obtain your prayer.

OEDIPUS

You consent then?

CREON

What I do not mean, I do not use to say.

OEDIPUS

Now lead me away from here.

CREON

Let go the children, then, and come.

OEDIPUS

Do not take them from me.

CREON

Do not seek to be master in everything,
for the things you mastered did not follow you throughout
    your life.

(As Creon and Oedipus go out.)

CHORUS

You that live in my ancestral Thebes, behold this
    Oedipus,—
him who knew the famous riddles and was a man most mas-
    terful;
not a citizen who did not look with envy on his lot—
See him now and see the breakers of misfortune swallow
    him!
Look upon that last day always. Count no mortal happy till
he has passed the final limit of his life secure from pain.

EURIPIDES: *HIPPOLYTUS*

INTRODUCTION

IT IS a commonplace to say that any great play admits of many analyses, that by reason of its greatness it has a many-sided interpretation. Some of these analyses may represent more accurately the intention of the artist, and some more perceptively the aspects of the work which are of predominant importance at the time when it appears. Only a moderate certainty can be attained as to the artist's original purpose, but whatever certainty there is comes from the attempt to explain the play in the light of its internal structure. We must at all costs avoid an interpretation based on what we believe the artist should have wanted to express. It is with this in mind that I put forward an interpretation of the *Hippolytus* widely at variance with the traditional view in the never extensive criticism to which the play has been subjected in the last sixty years.

This traditional criticism exhibits two main lines of agreement: (1) That the play is a symbolic conflict of two ideals, an austere chastity and the natural desires of the flesh. According to these critics, the manner in which the play is framed by the two goddesses, Aphrodite and Artemis, is significant. (2) That Hippolytus is the central figure. Phaedra, we are told, is merely the foil to Hippolytus—the means used to serve Aphrodite's vengeance. I believe it is possible to show that, first of all, the critics have misinterpreted the symbolism: it is a conflict, but not such a one as they envisage; and, second, this conflict centers around Phaedra, not Hippolytus, and the role of the latter is secondary.

There is one slightly different point of view on the subject matter significant enough to merit notice. This agrees with tradition already mentioned in regarding the play as a symbolic conflict between chastity and desire but believes that for a Greek the character of Hippolytus would be nothing in

itself admirable but stresses that the Greeks, being a healthy
and "natural" folk, would readily conceive that Hippolytus
was aiming at a degree of inhuman virtue which was in fact
a sin. It was a blasphemy against the nature of man. Hippolytus is an offender against the principle of "nothing too
much." Now it is true that Hippolytus does hold to the
spiritual chastity of the ascetic. It is true that he is insolent
both in his presumption in refusing to participate in the
worship of Aphrodite and in his treatment of the old servant
who gives him the advice of common sense. But it is equally
true that his punishment does not arise from any action of
his within the play's scope which can be regarded as typical
of his ascetic regimen. A man may be quite normally un-
chaste and refuse to go to bed with his father's wife.

There is a strong analogy between this story and that of
Bellerophon, and both in turn are comparable to the Joseph
tale in the Old Testament. In all three cases chastity, however desirable in itself, is reinforced by another sanction. In
the *Stheneboia* this sanction is the sacred duty of hospitality.
The guest must not corrupt the wife of the man who has fed
him and given him shelter. In the Joseph story the servant
must not corrupt the wife of the master who has been kind to
him. But the chastity of Hippolytus is tried in circumstances
where sin is double sin of the most obnoxious kind. In the
first place, yielding will involve a shameful breach of loyalty
to his father, and that aspect of the offense is already enough
to take it out of the category of venial slips which some believe to have been the hallmark of "humanism" among the
Greeks. But, in addition, there is the unsavory nature of the
relation to his father's wife. We have only to recall the case
of Phoenix in the *Iliad* (ix. 448), who was smitten with the
curse of sterility for the much less heinous offense of violating
his father's concubine. There were the most extenuating circumstances—he sinned at the request of his mother, in order
to break Amyntor's attachment to the woman; but, nonetheless, his father called the Furies against him, and he was
driven forth, condemned henceforth to childlessness. That
the Furies are called on is highly significant. They are sum-

moned as "upholders of the moral order and avengers of sins against the family" (Leaf). It is hardly hypercritical to suppose that the feeling which prompted Amyntor to curse his son was not only the wrath of outraged parenthood. Gen. 35:22 and 49:4 and the story of Absalom, who went in unto David's concubines in the sight of all Israel and thereby made these unhappy ladies to be regarded as permanently unclean, are other examples of the feeling awakened by this particular relation in the most various communities. Only fifteen years ago, in Eugene O'Neill's *Desire under the Elms*, we find the same theme treated again, and again there is the undertone of suppressed horror throughout the play.

Listen to what the Chorus (p. 185) says when they first hear of Phaedra's love. We notice the force of the adjective "unheard of" and the allusion to Phaedra's Cretan parentage. There is further proof if we look at the scene between the Nurse and Phaedra, where the latter is trying to express her unspeakable love. We find her making various indirect approaches to the subject: on page 183 she speaks of the tragic loves of the tragic Cretan household, beginning with Pasiphaë's unnatural passion for the bull.

All this is designed to lead the Nurse on to a correct guess at the frightfulness of the disclosure Phaedra is about to make concerning her own life. However, the Nurse is intentionally or unintentionally obtuse, and Phaedra tries another tack (p. 184).

> PHAEDRA: What is this thing, this love, of which they speak?
> NURSE: Sweetest and bitterest, both things in one, at once.
> PHAEDRA: One of the two, the bitterness, I've known.
> NURSE: Are you in love, child? And who is he?
> PHAEDRA: There is a man, ... his mother was an Amazon.....
> NURSE: You mean *Hippolytus?*
> PHAEDRA: You have spoken it, not I.

It is extremely important that there are no signs of any excessive horror on the part of the Nurse until Hippolytus' name is actually mentioned. Probably she is not exactly unused to affairs of this kind. What ultimately produces the outburst on page 185 is the appalling nature of the liaison. And, when the Nurse curses the daylight and the sun (p. 185), we can be sure that this will be the reaction of almost any right-minded member of the audience, if apprised of a similar monstrosity. Let us note Theseus' reactions when he learns of the crime which he believes has been committed.

p. 206   Hippolytus has dared to rape my wife.
         He has dishonoured God's holy sunlight.
p. 208   Come, you could stain your conscience with the impurity.
         Show me your face, show it to me, your father.

Had Euripides wished to give us in Hippolytus a symbolic figure whose efforts to achieve a superhuman virtue resulted in tragic disaster, it would have been easy to shape another play like the *Bacchae* with application to the sexual theme. Pentheus represents the cause of human reason struggling against primitive mysticism. He is one of the tragic fools of the world pitted hopelessly against the emotional forces which lie in the hinterland of man's nature, a man who believes that the world is run rationally as Euripides insists that it is not. But the essence of the difference of the two ideals crystallizes in the conflict. If Pentheus had permitted the establishment of the Dionysiac dances in Thebes and if he had permitted his father and the seer to attend them without let or hindrance, then there would have been no tragedy of Pentheus. Pentheus possesses qualities of fair-mindedness and justice which his opponent Dionysus signally lacks, but this is Euripides presenting the case with the objectivity of a great artist. The fact remains that Pentheus' tragedy is the direct result of his character exhibited in a typical aspect by the play's action. Now let us look at Hippolytus. If the last view mentioned above is right, we have to believe that the audience was bound to survey Hippolytus' position with the feeling, "That is precisely the attitude a wrong-headed fanatic like Hippolytus would assume." We must believe that the audience would consider an alternative open to him. Can we possibly imagine that any Greek would consider it a reasonable or natural action to consent to such a proposal as Phaedra makes to Hippolytus?

Well, then, we say that he is doomed from the beginning of the play. Yes, doomed, but doomed for what he is when the play opens. We assume Aphrodite's hatred as the dynamic force of the plot, and the rest follows. The goddess destroys her enemy by a peculiarly cruel and malicious device. He, the supremely chaste, must meet his ruin through suspicion of the greatest pollution. Nothing in his actions from the time the play opens helps or hinders the fulfilment of that design. Aphrodite has resolved to destroy him, and destroyed he is. And the moral symbolism, what of that? The moral symbolism is that Aphrodite and Artemis, the spirit of lust and the spirit of virginity, are opposed. Like Horatio, we may say: "There needs no ghost come from the grave to tell us that." A symbolic play, a play symbolic of the conflict of ideals, must in its action show how these ideals come into conflict. You cannot postulate their conflict and then contemplate their incompatibility through five acts relieved by episodes in themselves interesting but irrelevant to the thesis of the piece.

Suppose, then, that we abandon the theory that the play is a piece of moral symbolism and take up the position that it is concerned with the tragedy of Hippolytus, without any conflict of moral values. We are now regarding Hippolytus, like Oedipus, as a character tragically doomed from the outset by reason of a flaw in himself or an accidental fault. But the tragedy of Oedipus is actually a prolonged recognition, *anagnorisis*, as Aristotle would call it. The entire play is concerned with the king's discovery of himself and the tragic consequences of that discovery. That is, every action of Oedipus within the play conduces directly to the final catastrophe. Oedipus is active throughout as the instrument of his own ruin. But Hippolytus is completely passive. Apart from his expressed contempt for Aphrodite—and that belongs as much to the antecedents of the play as the murder of Laius in the *Oedipus*—and his rejection of Phaedra, which we cannot regard as a symptom of Hippolytus' peculiar weakness, the only positive attitude taken by Hippolytus is in the matter of the oath. Of this, more later.

Let us turn to the respective importance of the two figures, Phaedra and Hippolytus. The first thing that must strike the impartial observer is the respective length of the two parts. Admittedly, this is not decisive. We are not trying to weigh tragedy like meat, as Aristophanes says. But investigation of the Phaedra scenes is convincing by more than the mere matter of dead weight. Let us make a brief survey of the play, with the object of illuminating the spiritual proportions of the two parts.

It may be claimed that the Prologue, by its statement of the plot, gives decisive evidence that Hippolytus is the center of the play. The goddess Aphrodite, in her exposé of the circumstances antecedent to the play's action and of its subsequent course, starts with the story of Hippolytus' sin. She is bent on his punishment, and we are led to infer that she is principally moved by jealousy of Artemis. She relates how Phaedra first met Hippolytus, and how she sickened with love for him. She stresses the misery of Phaedra and tells us its ultimate consequence in Hippolytus' death brought about by his father Theseus' curse. When she says, "Phaedra shall die gloriously, but die she must. I do not rate her death so high that I should let my enemies go free and pay me not the retribution which honor demands that I have," she is not assigning Phaedra an inferior role in the play. She is merely explaining why it is necessary that one who is guiltless should perish in the course of the punishment exacted from Hippolytus. I do not seek to prove that the legend did not stress Hippolytus' punishment but that Euripides, taking the legend—and this playbill Prologue is only a restatement of the legend—changes the emphasis from Hippolytus to Phaedra.

After the Prologue with which the play opens, there is the song of the hunters in honor of Artemis. The scene which introduces Hippolytus is poignant in its suppressions and tragic irony. The following dialogue between him and the old servant marks out clearly the contours of his personality. He is youthfully imperious, a mystic, and piously confident in his own righteousness. At this point Euripides undoubtedly focuses our attention on him. It is more than likely that the dramatist is thinking of many of his young contemporaries, intellectual mystics with leanings toward Orphism.

After the lyrical chorus comes the story of Phaedra's love for Hippolytus. For five hundred lines from page 174 Hippolytus does not appear. He is not even kept before our eyes by the dialogue between the Nurse and Phaedra, for these scenes are clinical in their concentration on the symptoms of love and philosophical in their general treatment of the problem. Except for the *Electra* later, Euripides has made no more brilliant analysis of a woman's emotions. His subject, however, is a woman's emotions, not a woman. A passage in a letter from D. H. Lawrence to Garnett illustrates what I mean:

Somehow that which is physic, non-human in humanity, is more interesting to me than the old-fashioned human element which causes one to conceive a character in a certain moral scheme and make him consistent. The certain moral scheme is what I object to. . . . . When Marinetti writes: "It is the solidity of a blade of steel that is interesting in itself, that is the incomprehending and inhuman alliance of its molecules in resistance to, say, a bullet. The heat of a piece of wood or iron is a fact more passionate for us than the laughter or tears of a woman"—I know what he means. He is stupid as an artist for contrasting the heat of the iron and the laughter of a woman. Because what is interesting in the laughter of a woman is the same as the binding of the molecules of steel. It is the inhuman will, call it physiology, or, like Marinetti, physiology of matter if you like, which fascinates me. I do not care so much for what the woman feels in the ordinary sense of the word. That presumes an ego to feel with. I only care what the woman *is*, inhumanly, physiologically, materially according to the use of the word.[1]

It is the physiology of matter that fascinates Euripides. Phaedra's guilty innocence is a true example of the driving force of Marinetti's "inhuman will." How applicable to

[1] *Letters of D. H. Lawrence* (London: Heinemann, 1932), pp. 198–99. Acknowledgment is due to Mrs. Frieda Lawrence, William Heinemann, Ltd., and the Viking Press for permission to reprint this passage.

Euripides' treatment of Phaedra are these words of Lawrence we can see by contrasting the play with Seneca's
Hippolytus and Racine's *Phèdre;* both the Roman and the
Frenchman are trying to conceive a character within a certain moral scheme. For Seneca it is the deathly conventionality of the literary heroine of tragedy, a conventionality
bred of the rhetoric of the schools. For Racine it is the classic
artificiality of the seventeenth century, with its cumbrous
amorous and chivalrous pretensions. It is Euripides who
cares about the "something that is physic, non-human in
humanity."

In the scene from page 194 to page 197 we get a glimpse, a
significant glimpse, of Hippolytus. It is his pathological an-
tifeminist outburst. Apart from the revelation granted us of
his horror at such a proposal as the Nurse has made him, the
scene is indicative of a hopelessly neurotic mentality on the
part of Hippolytus. Whether there are really any grounds
for believing that this play was written at the time when
Euripides was involved in domestic trouble we have no
means of being sure. Aristophanes in the *Frogs* affirms that
Euripides had such trouble in his life, and he mentions it
directly after his criticism of the two plays, the *Stheneboia* and
the *Hippolytus*. There is also a strong tradition in the scholia
that the *Hippolytus* was composed at the moment of Euripides' bitterness. There seems, indeed, no very good reason
for disregarding this story. However that may be, the passage from page 196 to page 197 is the final refutation,
if another is needed, of the conception of Hippolytus as
a man free from any abnormality. On pages 208–9 (in
Theseus' indictment of his son) there are clear proofs that
Hippolytus, so far from being the healthy hero of the drama,
is someone haunted and tortured by an obsession. Homo-
sexuality would have been no particular reproach for a
young man like Hippolytus, but Euripides is searching to express something much deeper. It is the pathetic discontent,
restlessness, and supreme unhappiness of an adolescent over-
intellectually developed.

After the disappearance of Phaedra, the individual part

of the play is over. There remains the denouement of the plot, which is characterized by a certain stiff formality. The personal qualities which picked out the various shades in Hippolytus in the first scene are lost; and, in the charge and refutation scenes between him and Theseus, the matter and manner are mostly stock sophistic technique. Much of it recurs in the *agones* in the other plays (cf. p. 207 with *Hecuba* 816; p. 208 with *Medea* 516; p. 209 with *Troades* 969). Hippolytus' speech (p. 211) is all too evidently modeled on the speech of Creon in *Oedipus rex*, a play written shortly before this, the second version of the *Hippolytus*. But Creon's speech in the *Oedipus* (p. 112) seems realistic and characteristic, because Sophocles has by minor hints prepared us for just such a speech from a man of Creon's temperament. Hippolytus is accused in a very complicated emotional situation. He is also by no means a hard-headed pragmatist like Creon in the Sophoclean play. The man who could utter the denunciation of woman in the scene on page 196 would have been quite incapable of reasoning with this pretty attention to arguments of first and second worth, when charged with a most heinous crime by a father he dearly loved. All this scene shows Euripides in his customary role of rhetorical speech-writer. And as in the *Andromache* and the *Hecuba*, the *agon*[2] is an abstract *agon* in which for convenience the characters bear the same labels as when we saw them earlier in the play. But of the character of Hippolytus, the hot-headed Hippolytus who is arrogant with a servant who gives him a word or two of good advice, of the passionate Hippolytus hissing the words of hate at the Nurse, of the intensely devotional Hippolytus devoured with the white heat of his adoration of Artemis, there is not one trace. The only particular as distinct from the general formal characteristics which distinguish this *agon*

[2] The *agon* is the technical term for the contest in a Greek tragedy. Sometimes this contest is a clash between the characters in a purely verbal way and sometimes it is accompanied with at least the threat of physical violence. It was a fixed feature of both Greek tragedy and comedy and perhaps is rooted in some primitive religious rite which was part of the ceremony out of which tragedy and comedy sprang.

from the others is the audience' awareness that Hippolytus
is sacrificing himself for the sake of his oath. Hippolytus
swears to the Nurse that he will not reveal the secret she
confides in him. Later, since he realizes that the oath was
taken in ignorance, he is in doubt about the advisability of
keeping it but sticks to his word and perishes. Now, is this
the tragic element in his character? Is this the destruction of
the noble man through his greatest nobility? I think that
our answer lies in Hippolytus' own words. At the last moment, when he has heard his doom from Theseus, he specu-
lates on the wisdom of renouncing his oath and clarifying
the situation. "But no," he says, "he would not believe
who should believe and I should be false to my oath
and all for nothing." Surely it is plain that the oath is the
creation of the second edition and is designed to meet a
dramaturgical need. In the first edition,[3] where Phaedra
made the proposition to Hippolytus herself and survived his
death brought on him by her accusations, I doubt if there
was this oath. Then the *agon* may well have been Phaedra
and Hippolytus before Theseus. But when the tragedy demands that the truth should break on Theseus like a lightning bolt in the Epilogue, the oath which binds the lips of
Hippolytus is the only device whereby this can be accom-
plished. For a modern dramatist there would be no need for
such an oath. That one should not kiss and tell, or indeed
should not even tell where one has not kissed, is our heritage
from the Romantic age. But, like the oath imposed on the
Chorus by Phaedra, Hippolytus' oath and his fidelity to it
are of purely dramaturgical and not spiritual significance.
It is a necessary condition of the plot.

What follows the end of the *Hippolytus agon* is also con-

[3] There were two editions of the *Hippolytus*. The first version, when
acted, proved so unpalatable to the audience that they hissed it off the
stage. Apparently, Euripides had allowed Phaedra to make her offer
to Hippolytus herself and thus outraged the Athenians' sense of de-
cency. In the second version the Nurse was introduced to perform this
part, and it would seem that certain other minor changes, rather difficult to understand exactly, were also introduced. The evidence for this
story is to be found in Aristophanes' *Frogs*.

ventionally formal—a messenger's speech and the *theo-phaneia*. Here, then, we have our materials for forming a judgment on Hippolytus—two short opening scenes in which the dramatist adumbrates a character by sketching a few personal traits, Hippolytus' outburst against women, and one or two deductions to be made from Theseus' charges against him (pp. 208–9), e.g., that he was interested in Orphism; that he was spiritually arrogant; that he was a master of the supersophistical subtleties of argument. Can one, from such evidence as this, build either a picture of the ideal champion of chastity or the central figure of a great tragedy? It seems to me that it is Hippolytus who is the foil of Phaedra. Such personal traits as have been given him are designed to make of him a satire on the intellectuals of the fifth century.

What, then, at last shall we say is the theme of the *Hippolytus?* It is a play about the unchallengeable rule of love over the human animal and about the transformation which love can make in the human animal. In Aphrodite, Euripides has made a composite figure out of two different aspects of the goddess. One is the Aphrodite of folk tale, the petulant, wilful goddess of the *Iliad*. The other is the primitive life-force. As the first she furnishes the machinery of the plot, and part of that machinery is her hatred of Hippolytus and her destruction of him. It is Aphrodite, the life-force, who gives inner significance to the drama. It is her supremacy that the play asserts, but over Phaedra primarily and only secondarily over Hippolytus. Phaedra is a normal, rather conventional woman metamorphosed into a neurotic sadist. She can cast aside the moral restraints of the society in which she lives and try to seduce her stepson. When she fails, she plans his murder and makes her suicide the guaranty of his guilt (pp. 205–6). Yet, says Euripides, she is not really a criminal. Love is a frenzy of madness, and, when it strikes, the victim is not accountable in terms of her former personality or in terms of abstract rightness or wrongness. Thus, the general philosophical theme of the play, which centers around Phaedra, is crossed by the purely per-

sonal tragedy of Hippolytus. He, pathetically immature, un-
real, and more than a little of a prig, is precisely a man born
to be ill used by life in grotesque fashion. There is a grinning
cynicism in the description of this pure, young idealist who
knows nothing of love "save what I have heard or what I
have seen in pictures" (p. 210). But the legend has all
along identified him as Aphrodite's victim, and Euripides
only needed to draw a verisimilar detail or two to finish off
the picture. But the dramatist's own contribution (and one
of his most masterly achievements in characterization and
dramatic technique) is the study of Phaedra—this simple
and cowardly woman transformed into an incestuous harlot
and a murderess. On her he has spent the most pains and
virtually all the dramatic tension of the play. If Phaedra and
her tragedy are not his central interest, the artist has
been guilty of an incredible preoccupation with the non-
essential and an unintelligible concentration on irrelevant
detail. Just as the sacrifice of Alcestis for her husband has
been made the peg on which Euripides has hung a play
about the complacent selfishness of Admetus, the Torvald
Helmer of antiquity, so the story of Hippolytus done to
death by Aphrodite is the formal scheme into which the
study of Phaedra and her guilty innocence is fitted. Consider the following passages of the play and their context.
They are indications of the poet's stress.

The Nurse, on learning of her mistress' passion for Hippolytus says (p. 185):

> The chaste, they love not vice of their own will,
> but yet they love it. Cypris, you are no God:
> you are something stronger than God if that can be.
> You have ruined her and me and all the house.

On page 188, when she is pleading with Phaedra for the grati-
fication of love which otherwise threatens to destroy her life,
she says:

> The tide of love,
> at its full surge, is not withstandable.
> Upon the yielding spirit she comes gently,
> but to the proud and fanatic heart

she is a torturer with the brand of shame.
She wings her way through the air: she is in the sea,
in its foaming billows: from her everything,
that is, is born. For she engenders us,
and sows the seed of desire whereof we're born,
all we her children, living on the earth.

In view of the general philosophical character of the Nurse's speeches (cf. pp. 177 and 179), these two speeches have obviously more than dramaturgical importance.

On page 191, when the Nurse has won her case with Phaedra and Phaedra has yielded to her fatal pleading, the Chorus chants:

Love distills desire upon the eyes,
love brings bewitching grace into the heart
of those he would destroy.
I pray that Love may never come to me
with murderous intent,
in rhythms measureless and wild.
Not fire nor star have stronger bolts
than those of Aphrodite sent
by the hand of Eros, Zeus' child.

Finally, the Chorus sums up the action of the play before the *theophaneia* in the following lyric (p. 220):

Cypris, you guide men's hearts
and the inflexible
heart of the Gods and with you
comes Love with the flashing wings,
comes Love with the swiftest of wings.
Over the land he flies
and the land echoing salt sea.
He bewitches and maddens the heart
of the victim he swoops upon.
He bewitches the race of the mountain-haunting
lion and beasts of the sea,
and all the creatures that earth feeds,
and the blazing sun sees,—
and man, too,—
over all you hold kingly power,
Love, you are only ruler
over all these.

The two editions of the play give us a further indication of its author's interests. In the first, Phaedra makes the proposition to Hippolytus herself. That proved too much for the Athenian audience, so Euripides took it back and amended it. But he did not alter anything essential in the character of his main figure. He invented the Nurse as a go-between to carry out the ugly part of the affair. But there is no doubt whatever that Phaedra knows what is going on. That we can see from the conclusion of the scene between the Nurse and Phaedra (p. 191). Euripides wished to show that, given the most incriminating indictment of Phaedra possible, she is still innocent at the bar of human, if not divine, justice. Love working through Phaedra destroys Hippolytus. Such is the framework of the plot. But how does it work? With great dexterity the first Phaedra scene makes us feel all the subconscious stirrings of her mind before Phaedra herself is aware of them. Then the tentative approach to the step which will inevitably lead to her destruction. We are shown dramatically by the action in the first two scenes what Phaedra tells us explicitly later (pp. 186 and 187). Phaedra is guiltless, if by guilt we mean the conscious and deliberate choice of evil when the good is intellectually apprehended. But can we ever talk of a conscious decision of this kind when the chooser is under the influence of an essentially animal passion which carries him or her out and beyond the limits of reason? "I will show you," says Artemis to Theseus when she explains the machinery of the plot, "the frenzied love which seized your wife, or, I may call it, a noble innocence. For that most hated goddess, hated by all of us whose joy is virginity, drove her with love's sharp prickings to desire your son."

"Was the story I composed about Phaedra not true?" asks Euripides in the *Frogs*, where she is listed among his perverse creations along with Stheneboia. And the Athenian audience, as well as we, can answer as did Aeschylus: "By Zeus, most true," even if we do not continue with Aeschylus, "but the poet should conceal the vile, and not bring it on the boards. For children have the school master and the young men have the poets."

HIPPOLYTUS

* * *

PROLOGUE

APHRODITE

I am called the Goddess Cypris:
I am mighty among men and they honor me by many
  names.
All those that live and see the light of sun
from Atlas' Pillars to the tide of Pontus
are mine to rule.
Such as worship my power in all humility,
I exalt in honor.
But those whose pride is stiff-necked against me
I lay by the heels.
There is joy in the heart of a God also
when honored by men.

Now I will quickly tell you the truth of this story.

Hippolytus, son of Theseus by the Amazon,
pupil of Holy Pittheus,
alone among the folk of this land of Troezen has blasphemed
  me
counting me vilest of the Gods in Heaven.
He will none of the bed of love nor marriage,
but honours Artemis, Zeus' daughter,
counting her greatest of the Gods in Heaven
he is with her continually, this Maiden Goddess, in the
  greenwood.
They hunt with hounds and clear the land of wild things,
mortal with immortal in companionship.
I do not grudge him such privileges: why should I?
But for his sins against me
I shall punish Hippolytus this day.

I have no need to toil to win my end:
much of the task has been already done.

Once he came from Pittheus' house[1] to the country of
     Pandion
that he might see and be initiate in the holy mysteries.
Phaedra saw him
and her heart was filled with the longings of love.
This was my work.
So before ever she came to Troezen
close by the rock of Pallas in view of this land,
she dedicated a temple to Cypris.
For her love, too, dwelt in a foreign land.
Ages to come will call this temple after him, (*she points to
     where the temple stood above the Dionysiac Theater where our
     performance was taking place*),
the temple of the Goddess established here.
When Theseus left the land of Cecrops,
flying from the guilty stain of the murder of the Pallantids,
condemning himself to a year's exile
he sailed with his wife to this land.
Phaedra groans in bitterness of heart
and the goads of love prick her cruelly,
and she is like to die.
But she breathes not a word of her secret and none of the
     servants
know of the sickness that afflicts her.

[1] "Pittheus' house": The historian Pausanias, relating the legend
of Hippolytus says: "King Theseus, when he married Phaedra, daughter of the King of Crete, was in a quandary what to do with Hippolytus, his son by his former mistress, Antiope the Amazon. He did not
wish that after his own death Hippolytus should rule the children of
his legitimate marriage, nor yet that Hippolytus should be ruled by
them, for he loved him. So he sent the boy to be brought up by his
grandfather Pittheus who lived in Troezen and ruled there. Theseus
hoped that when Pittheus died Hippolytus might inherit the kingdom,
and thus peace within the family be preserved, Hippolytus governing
Troezen, and Phaedra's children holding sway in Athens." "Pandion's
country" and "land of Cecrops" both signify Attica. Pandion and
Cecrops were early legendary heroes of Attica.

But her love shall not remain thus aimless and unknown.
I will reveal the matter to Theseus and all shall come out.
Father shall slay son with curses,—
this son that is hateful to me.
For once the Lord Poseidon, Ruler of the Sea,
granted this favour to Theseus
that three of his prayers to the God should find answer.
Renowned shall Phaedra be in her death, but none the less
die she must.
Her suffering does not weigh in the scale so much
that I should let my enemies go untouched
escaping payment of that retribution
that honour demands that I have.
Look, here is the son of Theseus, Hippolytus!
He has just left his hunting.
I must go away.
See the great crowd that throngs upon his heels
and shouts the praise of Artemis in hymns!
He does not know
that the doors of death are open for him,
that he is looking on his last sun.

SCENE I

(*Enter Hippolytus, attended by friends and servants carrying nets, hunting spears, etc.*)

HIPPOLYTUS

Follow me singing
the praises of Artemis,
Heavenly One, Child of Zeus,
Artemis!
We are the wards of your care.

(*The Chorus of Huntsmen chant:*)

Hail, Holy and Gracious!
Hail Daughter of Zeus!
Hail Maiden Daughter of Zeus and Leto!
Dweller in the spacious sky!
Maid of the Mighty Father!

Maid of the Golden Glistening House!
Hail!
Maiden Goddess most beautiful of all the Heavenly Host
    that lives in Olympus!

(*Hippolytus advances to the altar on the right of the stage, the altar of
        Artemis, and lays a garland on it, praying:*)

My Goddess Mistress, I bring you ready woven
this garland. It was I that plucked and wove it,
plucked it for you in your Inviolate Meadow.
No shepherd dares to feed his flock within it:
no reaper plies a busy scythe within it:
only the bees in springtime haunt the Inviolate Meadow.
Its gardener is the Spirit Reverence who
refreshes it with water from the river.
Not those who by instruction have profited
to learn, but in whose very soul the seed
of Chastity towards all things alike
nature has deeply rooted, they alone
may gather flowers there! the wicked may not.

Loved mistress, here I offer you this coronal;
it is a true worshipper's hand that gives it you
to crown the golden glory of your hair.
With no man else I share this privilege
that I am ever with you and to your words
can answer words. True, I may only hear:
I may not see God face to face.
I pray that with such sweet companionship
my chariot wheels may graze the ultimate mark
set at the finish of life's stadium
even as I began the race.

SERVANT

King,—for I will not call you "Master," that belongs
to the Gods only—, will you take good advice?

HIPPOLYTUS

Certainly I will take good advice. I am not a fool.

SERVANT

In men's communities one rule holds good,
do you know it, King?

HIPPOLYTUS

      Not I. What is this rule?

SERVANT

Men hate the haughty of heart who will not be
the friend of every man.

HIPPOLYTUS

        And rightly too:
For haughty heart breeds arrogant demeanour.

SERVANT

And affability wins favour, then?

HIPPOLYTUS

Abundant favour. Aye, and profit, too,
at little cost of trouble.

SERVANT

         Do you think
that it's the same among the Gods in Heaven?

HIPPOLYTUS

If we in our world and the Gods in theirs
know the same usages,—Yes.

SERVANT

      Then, King, how comes it
that for a holy Goddess you have not even
a word of salutation?

HIPPOLYTUS

        Which Goddess?
Be careful, or you will find that tongue of yours
may make a serious mistake.

SERVANT

      This Goddess here
who stands before your gates, the Goddess Cypris.

HIPPOLYTUS

I worship her,—but from a long way off,
for I am chaste.

SERVANT

          Yet she's a holy Goddess,
and fair is her renown throughout the world.

HIPPOLYTUS

Men make their choice: one man honours one God,
and one another.

SERVANT

          Well, good fortune guard you!
if you have the mind you should have.

HIPPOLYTUS

God of nocturnal prowess is not my God.

SERVANT

Honour the Gods, son; Gods are jealous of honour.

HIPPOLYTUS

Go, men, into the house and look to supper.
A plentiful table is an excellent thing
after the hunt. And you (*singling out two*) rub down
  my horses.
When I have eaten I shall exercise them.
For your Cypris here,—a long good bye to her!

      (*The old man is left standing alone on the stage.*
       He prays before the statue of Aphrodite.)

O Cypris Mistress, we must not imitate
the young men when they have such thoughts as these.
As fits a slave to speak, here at your image
I bow and worship. You should grant forgiveness
when one that has a young tempestuous heart
speaks foolish words. Seem not to hear them.
You should be wiser than mortals, being Gods.

(*Enter Chorus of women, servants in Phaedra's house.*)

Chorus

Strophe

There is a rock streaming with water,
whose source, men say, is Ocean,
and it pours from the heart of its stone a spring
where pitchers may dip and be filled.
My friend was there and in the river water
she dipped and washed the royal purple robes,
and spread them on the rock's warm back
where the sunbeams played.
It was from her I heard at first
of the news of my mistress' sorrow.

Antistrophe

She lies on her bed within the house,
within the house and fever wracks her
and she hides her golden head in fine spun robes.
This is the third day
she has eaten no bread
and her body is pure and fasting.
For she would willingly bring her life to anchor
at the end of its voyage
the gloomy harbour of death.

Strophe

Is it Pan's frenzy that possesses you
or is Hecate's madness upon you, maid?
Can it be the holy Corybantes,
or the mighty Mother who rules the mountains?
Are you wasted in suffering thus,
for a sin against Dictynna Queen of hunters
Are you perhaps unhallowed having offered
no sacrifice to her from taken victims?
For she goes through the waters of the Lake

NOTE: Limnae, the Lake, a district in Laconia, was the center of
the worship of Artemis in the Peloponnese. From it she is sometimes
called Limnaios, or Lady of the Lake.

can travel on dry land beyond the sea,
the eddying salt sea.

Antistrophe

Can it be that some other woman's love,
a secret love that hides itself from you,
has beguiled your husband
the son of Erectheus
our sovran lord, that prince of noble birth?
Or has some sailor from the shores of Crete
put in at this harbour hospitable to sailors,
bearing a message for our queen,
and so because he told her some calamity
her spirit is bound in chains of grief
and she lies on her bed in sorrow?

Epode

Unhappy is the compound of woman's nature;
the torturing misery of helplessness,
the helplessness of childbirth and its madness
are linked to it for ever.
My body too has felt this thrill of pain,
and I called on Artemis, Queen of the Bow;
she has my reverence always
as she goes in the company of the Gods.

Scene II

*(Enter the nurse, supporting Phaedra. Servants follow
carrying a couch and pillows.)*

NURSE

A weary thing is sickness and its pains!
What must I do now?
Here is light and air, the brightness of the sky.
I have brought out the couch on which you tossed
in fever,—here clear of the house.
Your every word has been to bring you out,
but when you're here, you hurry in again.
You find no constant pleasure anywhere
for when your joy is upon you, suddenly

you're foiled and cheated.
There's no content for you in what you have
for you're forever finding something dearer,
some other thing,—because you have it not.
It's better to be sick than nurse the sick.
Sickness is single trouble for the sufferer:
but nursing means vexation of the mind,
and hard work for the hands beside.
The life of man entire is misery:
he finds no resting place, no haven from calamity.
But something other dearer still than life
the darkness hides and mist encompasses;
we are proved luckless lovers of this thing
that glitters in the underworld: no man
can tell us of the stuff of it expounding
what is, and what is not: we know nothing of it.
Unpiloted we're helplessly adrift
upon a sea of legends, lies and fantasy.

PHAEDRA (*to the servants*)

Lift me up! Lift my head up! All the muscles
are slack and useless. Here, you, take my hands.
They're beautiful, my hands and arms!
Take away this hat! It is too heavy to wear.
Take it away! Let my hair fall free on my shoulders.

NURSE

Quiet, child, quiet! Do not so restlessly
keep tossing to and fro! It's easier
to bear an illness if you have some patience
you are a lady nobly born: remember
the spirit of a lady nobly born.
We all must suffer sometimes: we are mortal.

PHAEDRA

O,
if I could only draw from the dewy spring
a draught of fresh spring water!

If I could only lie beneath the poplars,
in the tufted meadow and find my rest there!

NURSE

Child, why do you rave so? There are others here.
Cease tossing out these wild demented words
whose driver is madness.

PHAEDRA

Bring me to the mountains! I *will* go to the mountains!
Among the pine trees where the huntsmen's pack
trails spotted stags and hangs upon their heels.
God, how I long to set the hounds on, shouting!
And poise the Thessalian javelin drawing it back,—
here where my fair hair hangs above the ear,—
I would hold in my hand a spear with a steel point.

NURSE

What ails you, child? What is this love of hunting,
and you a lady! Draught of fresh spring water!
Here, beside the tower there is a sloping ridge
with springs enough to satisfy your thirst.

PHAEDRA

Artemis mistress of the Salty Lake
mistress of the ring echoing to the racers' hoofs
if only I could gallop your level stretches,
and break Venetian colts!

NURSE

This is sheer madness,
that prompts such whirling frenzied senseless words.
Here at one moment you're afire with longing
to hunt wild beasts and you'd go to the hills,
and then again all your desire is horses,
horses on the sands beyond the reach of the breakers.
Indeed it would need to be a mighty prophet
to tell which of the Gods mischievously
jerks you from your true course and thwarts your wits!

PHAEDRA

O, I am miserable! What is this I've done?
Where have I strayed from the highway of good sense?
I was mad. It was the madness sent from some God
that caused my fall.
I am unhappy, so unhappy! Nurse,
cover my face again. I am ashamed
of what I said. Cover me up. The tears
are flowing and my face is turned to shame.
Rightness of judgment is bitterness to the heart.
Madness is terrible. It is better then,
that I should die and know no more of anything.

NURSE

There now, you are covered up. But my own body
when will death cover that? I have learned much
from my long life. The mixing bowl of friendship,
the love of one for the other must be tempered.
Love must not touch the marrow of the soul.
Our affections must be breakable chains that we
can cast them off or tighten them.
That one soul so for two should be in travail
as I for her, that is a heavy burden.
The practices of life most deep and true
trip us up more, they say, than bring us joy.
They're enemies to health. So I praise less
the extreme than temperance in everything.
The wise will bear me out.

CHORUS LEADER

Old woman, you are Phaedra's faithful nurse.
We can see that she is in trouble but the cause
that ails her is black mystery to us.
We would like to hear you tell us what is the matter.

NURSE

I have asked and know no more. She will not tell me.

CHORUS LEADER
Not even what began it?

NURSE
                    And my answer
Is still the same: of all this she will not speak.

CHORUS LEADER,
But see how ill she is, and how her body
is wracked and wasted!

NURSE
              Yes, she has eaten nothing
for two days now.

CHORUS LEADER
              Is this the scourge of madness?
Or can it be . . . . that death is what she seeks?

NURSE
Aye, death. She is starving herself to death.

CHORUS LEADER
I wonder that her husband suffers this.

NURSE
She hides her troubles, swears that she isn't sick.

CHORUS LEADER
But does he not look into her face and see
a witness that disproves her?

NURSE
              No, he is gone.
He is away from home, in foreign lands.

CHORUS LEADER
Why, you must force her then to find the cause
of this mind wandering sickness!

NURSE
                              Every means
I have tried and still have won no foot of ground.
But I'll not give up trying, even now.
You are here and can in person bear me witness
that I am loyal to my masters always
even in misfortune's hour.

> (*She approaches Phaedra, who has been lying mute
> under the coverlet and speaks coaxingly.*)

NURSE

Dear child, let us both forget our former words.
Be kinder, you: unknit that ugly frown.
For my part I will leave this track of thought:
I cannot understand you there. I'll take
another and a better argument.

If you are sick and it is some secret sickness,
here are women standing at your side to help.
But if your troubles may be told to men,
speak, that a doctor may pronounce upon it.
So, not a word! O, why will you not speak?
There is no remedy in silence, child.
Either I am wrong and then you should correct me:
or right, and you should yield to what I say.
Say something! Look at me!

Women, I have tried and tried and all for nothing.
We are as far as ever from our goal.
It was the same before. She was not melted
by anything I said. She would not obey me.

But this you shall know, though to my reasoning
you are more dumbly obstinate than the sea:
If you die, you will be a traitor to your children.
They will never know their share in a father's palace.
No, by the Amazon Queen, the mighty rider
who bore a master for your children, one

bastard in birth but true born son in mind
you know him well,—Hippolytus . . . .

     So that has touched you?

PHAEDRA
You have killed me, nurse. For God's sake, I entreat you,
never again speak that man's name to me.

NURSE
You see? You have come to your senses, yet despite that
you will not make your children happy nor
save your own life besides.

PHAEDRA
     I love my children.
It is another storm of fate that batters me.

NURSE
Your hands are clean,—there is no stain on them?

PHAEDRA
My hands are clean: the stain is in my heart.

NURSE
The hurt comes from outside? Some enemy?

PHAEDRA
One I love destroys me. Neither of us wills it.

NURSE
Has Theseus sinned a sin against you then?

PHAEDRA
God keep me equally guiltless in his sight!

NURSE
What is this terror urging you to death?

PHAEDRA
Leave me to my sins. My sins are not against you.

NURSE

Not of my will, but yours, you cast me off.

PHAEDRA

Would you force confession, my hand-clasping suppliant?

NURSE

Your knees too,—and my hands will never free you.

PHAEDRA

Sorrow, nurse, sorrow, you will find my secret.

NURSE

Can I know greater sorrow than losing you?

PHAEDRA

Entreat to death! My honour lies in silence.

NURSE

And then you will hide this honour, though I beseech you?

PHAEDRA

Yes, for I seek to win good out of shame.

NURSE

Where honour is, speech will make you more honourable.

PHAEDRA

O, God, let go my hand and go away!

NURSE

No, for you have not given me what you should.

PHAEDRA

I yield. Your suppliant hand compels my reverence.

NURSE

I will say no more. Yours is the word from now.

PHAEDRA

Unhappy mother, what a love was yours!

NURSE

It is her love for the bull you mean, dear child?

PHAEDRA

Unhappy sister, bride of Dionysus!

NURSE

Why these ill-boding words about your kin?

PHAEDRA

And I the unlucky third, see how I end!

NURSE

Your words are wounds. Where will your tale conclude?

PHAEDRA

Mine is an inherited curse. It is not new.

NURSE

I have not yet heard what I most want to know.

PHAEDRA

If you could say for me what I must say for myself.

NURSE

I am no prophet to know your hidden secrets.

PHAEDRA

What is this thing, this love, of which they speak?

NURSE

Sweetest and bitterest, both in one, at once.

PHAEDRA

One of the two, the bitterness, I've known.

NURSE

Are you in love, my child? And who is he?

PHAEDRA

There is a man, ... his mother was an Amazon . . . .

NURSE

You mean Hippolytus?

PHAEDRA

You

have spoken it, not I.

NURSE

What do you mean? This is my death.
Women, this is past bearing. I'll not bear
life after this. A curse upon the daylight!
A curse upon this shining sun above us!
I'll throw myself from a cliff, throw myself headlong!
I'll be rid of life somehow, I'll die somehow!
Farewell to all of you! This is the end for me.

The chaste, they love not vice of their own will,
but yet they love it. Cypris, you are no God.
You are something stronger than God if that can be.
You have ruined her and me and all this house.

(*The Nurse goes off.*)

(*The Chorus forms into two half-choruses.*)

FIRST HALF-CHORUS

Did you hear, did you hear
the queen crying aloud,
telling of a calamity
which no ear should hear?

SECOND HALF-CHORUS

I would rather die
than think such thoughts as hers.

FIRST HALF-CHORUS

I am sorry for her trouble.

SECOND HALF-CHORUS

Trouble nourishes mankind.

FIRST HALF-CHORUS (*turning to Phaedra*)
You are dead, you yourself
have dragged your ruin to the light
what can happen now in the long
dragging stretch of the rest of your days?

CHORUS (*united*)
We know now, we know now
how your love will end,
poor unhappy Cretan girl!

PHAEDRA
Hear me, you women of Troezen who live
in this extremity of land, this anteroom to Argos.
Many a time in night's long empty spaces
I have pondered on the causes of a life's shipwreck.
I think that our lives are worse than the mind's quality
would warrant. There are many who know virtue.
We know the good, we apprehend it clearly.
But we can't bring it to achievement. Some
are betrayed by their own laziness, and others
value some other pleasure above virtue.
There are many pleasures in a woman's life,—
long gossiping talks and leisure, that sweet curse.
Then there is shame that thwarts us. Shame is of two kinds.
The one is harmless, but the other a plague.
For clarity's sake, we should not talk of "shame,"
a single word for two quite different things.
These then are my thoughts. Nothing can now seduce me
to the opposite opinion. I will tell you
in my own case the track which my mind followed.
At first when love had struck me I reflected
how best to bear it. Silence was my first plan.
Silence and concealment. For the tongue
is not to be trusted: it can criticise
another's faults, but on its own possessor
it brings a thousand troubles.
Then I believed that I could conquer love,

conquer it with discretion and good sense.
And when that too failed me, I resolved to die.
And death is the best plan of them all. Let none of you
dispute that.
It would always be my choice
to have my virtues known and honoured. So
when I do wrong I could not endure to see
a circle of condemning witnesses.
I know what I have done: I know the scandal:
and all too well I know that I am a woman.
I could wish
the hatred of the world and a cruel death
upon the wife who herself plays the tempter
and stains her loyalty to her husband's bed
by dalliance with strangers. In the wives
of noble houses first this taint begins:
when wickedness approves itself to those
of noble birth, it will surely be approved
by their inferiors. Truly too I hate
lip-worshippers of chastity who own
a lecherous daring when they have privacy.
O Cypris, Sea-Born Goddess, how can they
look frankly in the faces of their husbands
and never shiver with fear lest their accomplice,
old darkness, and the rafters of the house
take voice and cry aloud?
This then, my friends, is my destruction:
I cannot bear that I should be discovered
a traitor to my husband and my children.
God grant them rich and glorious life in Athens,—
our famous Athens,—freedom in word and deed,
and from their mother an honourable name.
It makes the stoutest hearted man a slave
if in his soul he knows his parents' shame.

The proverb runs: "There is one thing alone
that stands the brunt of life throughout its course,
a quiet conscience," . . . . a just and quiet conscience
whoever can attain it.

Time is as diligent with his looking glass
as a young girl. He holds it up to us
and sometimes as occasion falls, he shows us
the ugly rogues of the world. I would not wish
that I should be seen among them.

CHORUS LEADER

How virtue is held lovely everywhere,
and harvests a good name among mankind!

(*The Nurse returns.*)

NURSE

Mistress, the trouble you have lately told me,
coming on me so suddenly, frightened me
but now I realize that I was foolish.
In this world second thoughts, it seems, are best.
Your case is not so extraordinary,
beyond thought or reason. The Goddess in her anger
has smitten you, and you are in love. What wonder
is this? There are many thousands suffer with you.
So, you will die for love! And all the others,
who love, and who will love, must they die, too?
How will that profit them? The tide of love,
at its full surge, is not withstandable.
Upon the yielding spirit she comes gently,
but to the proud and fanatic heart
she is a torturer with the brand of shame.
She wings her way through the air: she is in the sea,
in its foaming billows: from her everything,
that is, is born. For she engenders us,
and sows the seed of desire whereof we're born,
all we her children, living on the earth.
He who has read the writings of the ancients
and has lived much in books, he knows
that Zeus once loved the lovely Semele;
he knows that Dawn, the bright light of the world,
once ravished Cephalus hence to the God's Company

for love's sake. Yet all these dwell in heaven.
They are content, I am sure, to be subdued
by the stroke of love.
But you, you won't submit! Why, you should certainly
have had your father beget you on fixed terms
or with other Gods for masters, if you don't like
the laws that rule this world. Tell me, how many
of the wise ones of the earth do you suppose
see with averted eyes their wives turned faithless;
how many erring sons have fathers helped
with secret loves? It is the wise man's part
to leave in darkness everything that is ugly.

We should not in the conduct of our lives
be too exacting. Look, see this roof here,—
these overarching beams that span your house,—
could builders with all their skill lay them dead straight?
You've fallen into the great sea of love
and with your puny swimming would escape!
If in the sum you have more good luck than ill,
count yourself fortunate,—for you are mortal.

Come, dear, give up your discontented mood.
Give up your railing. It's only insolent pride
to wish to be superior to the Gods.
Endure your love. The Gods have willed it so.
You are sick. Then try to find some subtle means
to turn your sickness into health again.
There are magic love charms, spells of enchantment;
we'll find some remedy for your love-sickness.
Men would take long to hunt devices out,
if we the women did not find them first.

CHORUS LEADER

Phaedra, indeed she speaks more usefully
for to-day's troubles. But it is you I praise.
and yet my praise brings with it more discomfort
than her rebuke: it is bitterer to the ear.

PHAEDRA

This is the deadly thing which devastates
well-ordered cities and the homes of men,—
that's it, this art of over subtle words.
It's not the words ringing delight in the ear
that one should speak, but those that have the power
to save their hearer's honourable name.

NURSE

This is high moralizing! What you want
is not fine words, but the man! Come, let's be done.
And tell your story frankly and directly.
For if there were no danger to your life,
as now there is,—or if you could be prudent,
I never would have led you on so far,
merely to please your fancy or your lust.
But now a great prize hangs on our endeavours,
and that's the saving of a life,—yours, Phaedra,
there's none can blame us for our actions now.

PHAEDRA

What you say is wicked, wicked! Hold your tongue!
I will not hear such shameful words again.

NURSE

O, they are shameful! But they are better than
your noble sounding moral sentiments.
"The deed" is better if it saves your life:
than your "good name" in which you die exulting.

PHAEDRA

For God's sake, do not press me any further!
What you say is true, but terrible!
My very soul is subdued by my love
and if you plead the cause of wrong so well
I shall fall into the abyss
from which I now am flying.

NURSE

If that is what you think, you should be virtuous.
But if you are not, obey me: that is next best.
It has just come to my mind, I have at home
some magic love charms. They will end your trouble
they'll neither harm your honour nor your mind.
they'll end your trouble, ... only you must be brave.

PHAEDRA

Is this a poison ointment or a drink?

NURSE

I don't know. Don't be over-anxious, child,
to find out what it is. Accept its benefits.

PHAEDRA

I am afraid of you: I am afraid
that you will be too clever for my good.

NURSE

You are afraid of everything. What is it?

PHAEDRA

You surely will not tell this to Hippolytus?

NURSE

Come, let that be: I will arrange all well.
Only, my lady Cypris of the Sea,
be my helper you. The other plans I have
I'll tell to those we love within the house;
that will suffice.

CHORUS

Strophe

Love distills desire upon the eyes,
love brings bewitching grace into the heart
of those he would destroy.
I pray that love may never come to me
with murderous intent,
in rhythms measureless and wild.

Not fire nor stars have stronger bolts
than those of Aphrodite sent
by the hand of Eros, Zeus' child.

Antistrophe

In vain by Alpheus' stream,
in vain in the halls of Phoebus' Pythian shrine
the land of Greece increases sacrifice.
But Love the King of Men they honour not,
although he keeps the keys
of the temple of desire,
although he goes destroying through the world
author of dread calamities
and ruin when he enters human hearts.

Strophe

The Oechalian maiden who had never known
the bed of love, known neither man nor marriage
the Goddess Cypris gave to Heracles.
She took her from the home of Eurytus,
maiden unhappy in her marriage song,
wild as a Naiad or a Bacchanal,
with blood and fire, a murderous hymenaeal!

Antistrophe

O holy walls of Thebes and Dirce's fountain
bear witness you, to Love's grim journeying:
once you saw Love bring Semele to bed,
lull her to sleep, clasped in the arms of Death,
pregnant with Dionysus by the thunder king.
Love is like a flitting bee in the world's garden
and for its flowers, destruction is in his breath.

Scene III

*(Phaedra is standing listening near the central door
of the palace.)*

PHAEDRA

Women, be silent! *(She listens and then recoils.)*
O, I am destroyed for ever.

CHORUS LEADER
What is there terrible within the house?

PHAEDRA
Hush, let me hear the voices within!

CHORUS LEADER
And I obey. But this is sorrow's prelude.

PHAEDRA (*cries out*)
O, I am the most miserable of women!

> (*The Chorus Leader and the Chorus babble excitedly
> among themselves.*)

What does she mean by her cries?
Why does she scream?
Tell us the fear-winged word, Mistress, the fear-winged
    word,
rushing upon the heart.

PHAEDRA
I am lost. Go, women, stand and listen there yourselves
and hear the tumult that falls on the house.

CHORUS LEADER
Mistress, you stand at the door.
It is you who can tell us best
what happens within the house.

PHAEDRA
Only the son of the horse-loving Amazon,
Hippolytus, cursing a servant maid.

CHORUS LEADER
My ears can catch a sound,
but I can hear nothing clear.
I can only hear a voice
scolding in anger.

PHAEDRA

It is plain enough. He cries aloud against
the mischievous bawd who betrays her mistress' love.

CHORUS LEADER

Lady, you are betrayed!
How can I help you?
What is hidden is revealed.
You are destroyed.
Those you love have betrayed you.

PHAEDRA

She loved me and she told him of my troubles,
and so has ruined me. She was my doctor,
but her cure has made my illness mortal now.

CHORUS LEADER

What will you do? There is no cure.

PHAEDRA

I know of one, and only one,—quick death.
That is the only cure for my disease.

*(She retires into the palace through one of the side doors just as
    Hippolytus issues through the central door, dogged by the Nurse.
    Phaedra is conceived of as listening from behind her door dur-
    ing the entire conversation between the Nurse and Hippolytus.)*

HIPPOLYTUS

O Mother Earth! O Sun and open sky!
What words I have heard from this accursed tongue!

NURSE

Hush, son! Someone may hear you.

HIPPOLYTUS

You cannot
expect that I hear horror and stay silent.

NURSE

I beg of you, entreat you by your right hand,
your strong right hand, ... don't speak of this!

HIPPOLYTUS

Don't lay your hand on me! Let go my cloak!

NURSE

By your knees then, ... don't destroy me!

HIPPOLYTUS

What is this?
Don't you declare that you have done nothing wrong?

NURSE

Yes, but the story, son, is not for everyone.

HIPPOLYTUS

Why not? A pleasant tale makes pleasanter telling,
when there are many listeners.

NURSE

You will not break your oath to me, surely you will not?

HIPPOLYTUS

My tongue swore, but my mind was still unpledged.

NURSE

Son, what would you do?
You'll not destroy your friends?

HIPPOLYTUS

"Friends" you say!
I spit the word away. None of the wicked
are friends of mine.

NURSE

Then pardon, son. It's natural
that we should sin, being human.

HIPPOLYTUS

Women! This coin which men find counterfeit!
Why, why, Lord Zeus, did you put them in the world,
in the light of the sun? If you were so determined
to breed the race of man, the source of it
should not have been women. Men might have dedicated
in your own temples images of gold,
silver, or weight of bronze, and thus have bought
the seed of progeny, ... to each been given
his worth in sons according to the assessment
of his gift's value. So we might have lived
in houses free of the taint of women's presence.
But now, to bring this plague into our homes
we drain the fortunes of our homes. In this
we have a proof how great a curse is woman.
For the father who begets her, rears her up,
must add a dowry gift to pack her off
to another's house and thus be rid of the load.
And he again that takes the cursed creature
rejoices and enriches his heart's jewel
with dear adornment, beauty heaped on vileness.
With lovely clothes the poor wretch tricks her out
spending the wealth that underprops his house.
That husband has the easiest life whose wife
is a mere nothingness, a simple fool
uselessly sitting by the fireside.
I hate a clever woman,—God forbid
that I should ever have a wife at home
with more than woman's wits! Lust breeds mischief
in the clever ones. The limits of their minds
deny the stupid lecherous delights.
We should not suffer servants to approach them,
but give them as companions voiceless beasts,
dumb, ... but with teeth, that they might not converse,
and hear another voice in answer.
But now at home the mistress plots the mischief
and the maid carries it abroad. So you, vile woman,

came here to me to bargain and to traffic
in the sanctity of my father's marriage bed.
I'll go to a running stream and pour its waters
into my ear to purge away the filth.
Shall I who cannot even hear such impurity,
and feel myself untouched, ... shall I turn sinner?
Woman, know this. It is my piety saves you.
Had you not caught me off my guard and bound
my lips with an oath by heaven I would not refrain
from telling this to my father.
Now I will go and leave this house until
Theseus returns from his foreign wanderings.
and I'll be silent. But I'll watch you close.
I'll walk with my father step by step and see
how you look at him, ... you and your mistress both.
I have tasted of the daring of your infamy.
I'll know it for the future. Curses on you!
I'll hate you women, hate and hate and hate you,
and never have enough of hating. . . . .
                                        Some
say that I talk of this eternally,
yes, but eternal too is woman's wickedness.
Either let someone teach them to be chaste,
or suffer me to trample on them for ever.

(*Phaedra comes out from behind the door. Exit Hippolytus.*)

PHAEDRA

Bitter indeed is woman's destiny!
I have failed. What trick is there now, what cunning plea
to loose the knot around my neck?
I have had justice. O earth and the warm sunlight!
Where shall I escape from my fate?
How shall I hide my trouble?
What God or man would appear
to bear hand or part in my crime?
There is a limit to all suffering and I have reached it.
I am the unhappiest of women.

CHORUS

Alas, mistress, all is over now
your servant's schemes have failed and you are ruined.

(Enter the Nurse.)

PHAEDRA

This is fine service you have rendered me,
corrupted, damned seducer of your friends!
May Zeus, the father of my fathers' line,
blot you out utterly, raze you from the world
with thunderbolts! Did I not see your purpose,
did I not say to you, "Breathe not a word of this"
which now overwhelms me with shame? But you,
you did not hold back. And therefore I must die
and die dishonoured.
Enough of this. We have a new theme now.
The anger of Hippolytus is whetted.
He will tell his father all the story of your sin
to my disparagement. He will tell old Pittheus, too.
He will fill all the land with my dishonour.
May my curse
light upon you, on you and all the others
who eagerly help unwilling friends to ruin.

NURSE

Mistress, you may well blame my ill-success,
for sorrow's bite is master of your judgment.
But I have an answer to make if you will listen.
I reared you up. I am your loyal servant.
I sought a remedy for your love's sickness,
and found, ... not what I sought.
Had I succeeded, I had been a wise one.
Our wisdom varies in proportion to
our failure or achievement.

PHAEDRA

                    So, that's enough
for me? Do I have justice if you deal me
my death blow and then say "I was wrong: I grant it."

NURSE

We talk too long. True I was not wise then.
But even from this desperate plight, my child,
you can escape.

PHAEDRA
You, speak no more to me.
You have given me dishonourable advice.
What you have tried has brought dishonour too.
Away with you!
Think of yourself. For me and my concerns
I will arrange all well.

(*Exit Nurse.*)

You noble ladies of Troezen, grant me this,
this one request, that what you have heard here
you wrap in silence.

CHORUS LEADER

I swear by holy Artemis, child of Zeus,
never to bring your troubles to the daylight.

PHAEDRA

I thank you. I have found one single blessing
in this unhappy business, one alone,
that I can pass on to my children after me
life with an uncontaminated name,
and myself profit by the present throw
of Fortune's dice. For I will never shame you,
my Cretan home, nor will I go to face
Theseus, defendant on an ugly charge,
never,—for one life's sake.

CHORUS LEADER

What is the desperate deed you mean to do,
the deed past cure.

PHAEDRA
Death. But the way of it, that
is what I now must plan.

CHORUS LEADER
                    O, do not speak of it!
PHAEDRA

No, I'll not speak of it. But on this day
when I shake off the burden of this life
I shall delight the Goddess who destroys me,
the Goddess Cypris.
Bitter will have been the love that conquers me,
but in my death I shall at least bring sorrow,
upon another, too, that his high heart
may know no arrogant joy at my life's shipwreck;
he will have his share in this my mortal sickness
and learn of chastity in moderation.

CHORUS

   Strophe

Would that I were under the cliffs, in the secret hiding-
      places of the rocks,
that Zeus might change me to a winged bird
and set me among the feathered flocks.
I would rise and fly to where the sea
washes the Adriatic coast,
and to the waters of Eridanus.
Into that deep-blue tide,
where their father, the Sun, goes down,
the unhappy maidens weep
tears from their amber-gleaming eyes
in pity for Phaethon.

   Antistrophe

I would win my way to the coast,
apple-bearing Hesperian coast,
of which the minstrels sing.
Where the Lord of the Ocean
denies the voyager further sailing,
and fixes the solemn limit of Heaven
which Giant Atlas upholds.
There the streams flow with ambrosia

by Zeus' bed of love,
and holy earth, the giver of life,
yields to the Gods rich blessedness.

Strophe

O Cretan ship with the white sails,
from a happy home you brought her,
my mistress over the tossing foam, over the salty sea,
to bless her with a marriage unblest.
Black was the omen that sped her here,
black was the omen for both her lands,
for glorious Athens and her Cretan home,
as they bound to Munychia's pier
the cables' ends with their twisted strands
and stepped ashore on the continent.

Antistrophe

The presage of the omen was true;
Aphrodite has broken her spirit
with the terrible sickness of impious love.
The waves of destruction are over her head,
from the roof of her room with its marriage bed,
she is tying the twisted noose.
And now it is around her fair white neck!
The shame of her cruel fate has conquered.
She has chosen good name rather than life:
she is easing her heart of its bitter load of love.

NURSE (*within*)

Ho, there, help!
You who are near the palace, help!
My mistress, Theseus' wife, has hanged herself.

CHORUS LEADER

It is done, she is hanged in the dangling rope.
Our Queen is dead.

NURSE (*within*)

Quick! Someone bring a knife!
Help me cut the knot around her neck.

(*The Chorus talks among itself.*)

FIRST WOMAN

What shall we do, friends? Shall we cross the threshold,
and take the Queen from the grip of the tight-drawn cords?

SECOND WOMAN

Why should we? There are servants enough within
for that. Where hands are over busy,
there is no safety.

NURSE (*within*)

Lay her out straight, poor lady.
Bitter shall my lord find her housekeeping.

THIRD WOMAN

From what I hear, the queen is dead.
They are already laying out the corpse.

SCENE IV

(*Theseus enters.*)

THESEUS

Women, what is this crying in the house?
I heard heavy wailing on the wind,
as were servants, mourning. And my house
deigns me no kindly welcome though I come
crowned with good luck from Delphi.
The doors are shut against me. Can it be
something has happened to my father. He is old.
His life has travelled a great journey,
but bitter would be his passing from our house.

CHORUS LEADER

King, it is not the old who claim your sorrow.
Young is the dead and bitterly you'll grieve.

THESEUS

My children . . . . has death snatched a life away?

CHORUS LEADER
Your children live,—but sorrowfully, King.
Their mother is dead.

THESEUS
                It cannot be true, it cannot.
My wife! How could she be dead?

CHORUS LEADER
She herself tied the rope around her neck.

THESEUS
Was it grief and numbing loneliness drove her to it,
or has there been some violence at work?

CHORUS LEADER
I know no more than this. I, too, came lately
to mourn for you and yours, King Theseus.

THESEUS
O,
Why did I plait this coronal of leaves,
and crown my head with garlands, I the envoy
who find my journey end in misery.

                    (*To the servants within.*)

Open the doors! Unbar the fastenings,
that I may see this bitter sight, my wife
who killed me when she killed herself.

        (*The doors are opened, and Theseus goes inside. The Chorus
            in the Orchestra divide again into half-choruses and
                                chant.*)

FIRST HALF-CHORUS
Woman unhappy, tortured,
your suffering, your death,
has shaken this house to its foundations.

SECOND HALF-CHORUS

You were daring, you who died
in violence and guilt.
Here was a wrestling: your own hand against your life.

CHORUS (*united*)

Who can have cast a shadow on your life?

SCENE V

(*Enter Theseus.*)

THESEUS

O, city, city! Bitterness of sorrow!
Extremest sorrow that a man can suffer!
Fate, you have ground me and my house to dust,
fate in the form of some ineffable
pollution, some grim spirit of revenge.
The file has whittled away my life until
it is a life no more.
I am like a swimmer that falls into a great sea:
I cannot cross this towering wave I see before me.

My wife! I cannot think
of anything said or done to drive you to this horrible death.
You are like a bird that has vanished out of my hand.
You have made a quick leap out of my arms
into the land of Death.

It must be the sin of some of my ancestors in the dim past
God in his vengeance makes me pay now.

CHORUS LEADER

You are not the only one, King.
Many another as well as you
has lost a noble wife.

THESEUS

Darkness beneath the earth, darkness beneath the earth!
How good to lie there and be dead,
now that I have lost you, my dearest comrade.
Your death is no less mine.

(Turning furiously to the servants.)

Will any of you
Tell me what happened?
Or does the palace keep a flock of you for nothing?

God, the pain I saw in the house!
I cannot speak of it, I cannot bear it.
I cannot speak of it, I cannot bear it. I am a dead man.
My house is empty and my children orphaned.
You have left them, you
my loving wife,—
the best of wives
of all the sun looks down on or the blazing stars of the night.

CHORUS

Woe for the house! Such storms of ill assail it.
My eyes are wells of tears and overrun,
and still I fear the evil that shall come.

*(As the attendants are taking away the body, Theseus stops them.
He has seen clenched in Phaedra's hand a tablet with writing
on it. He takes and opens it.)*

THESEUS

What can she wish to tell me?
Have you written begging me to care
for our children or, in dumb entreaty,
about another woman? Sad one, rest confident.
There is no woman in the world who shall come to this house
and sleep by my side.
Look, the familiar signet ring,
hers who was once my wife!

(The Chorus of women speak singly.)

FIRST WOMAN

Surely some God
brings sorrow upon sorrow in succession.

Second Woman

The house of our lords is destroyed: it is no more.

Third Woman

God, if it so may be, hear my prayer.
Do not destroy this house utterly. I am a prophet:
I can see the omen of coming trouble.

Chorus Leader

What is it? Tell us if we may share the story.

Theseus

It cries aloud, this tablet, cries aloud,
and Death is its song!

Chorus Leader

Prelude of ruin!

Theseus

I shall no longer hold this secret prisoner
in the gates of my mouth. It is horrible,
yet I will speak.
Citizens,
Hippolytus has dared to rape my wife.
He has dishonoured God's holy sunlight.

(*He turns in the direction of the sea.*)

Father Poseidon, once you gave to me
three curses. . . . . Now with one of these, I pray,
kill my son. Suffer him not to escape,
this very day, if you have promised truly.

Chorus Leader

Call back your curses, King, call back your curses.
Else you will realise that you were wrong
another day, too late. I pray you, trust me.

Theseus

I will not. And I now make this addition:
I banish him from this land's boundaries.

So fate shall strike him, one way or the other,
either Poseidon will respect my curse,
and send him dead into the House of Hades,
or exiled from this land, a beggar wandering,
on foreign soil, his life shall suck the dregs
of sorrow's cup.

CHORUS LEADER

Here comes your son, and seasonably, King Theseus.
Give over your deadly anger. You will best
determine for the welfare of your house.

(*Enter Hippolytus with companions.*)
HIPPOLYTUS

I heard you crying, father, and came quickly.
I know no cause why you should be in mourning.
Tell me.
(*Suddenly he sees the body of Phaedra.*)

O father, father,—Phaedra! Dead! She's dead!
I cannot believe it. But a few moments since
I left her. . . . . And she is still so young.
But what could it be? How did she die, father?
I *must* hear the truth from you. Why won't you answer?

I always want to know of everything,
and when you are in trouble most of all.
You should not hide your troubles from your friends,
and, father, those who are closer than your friends.

THESEUS

What fools men are! You work and work for nothing,
you teach ten thousand tasks to one another,
invent, discover everything. One thing only
you do not know: one thing you never hunt for:—
a way to teach fools wisdom.

HIPPOLYTUS

Clever indeed
would be the teacher able to compel

the stupid to be wise! This is no time
for such fine logic chopping.
                    I am afraid
your tongue runs wild through sorrow.

THESEUS
                    If there were
some token now, some mark to make the division
clear between friend and friend, the true and the false!
All men should have two voices, one the just voice,
and one as chance would have it. In this way
the treacherous scheming voice would be confuted
by the just, and we should never be deceived.

HIPPOLYTUS
Some friend has poisoned your ear with slanderous tales.
Am I suspected, then, for all my innocence?
I am amazed. I am amazed to hear
your words. They are distraught. They go indeed
far wide of the mark!

THESEUS
The mind of man,—how far will it advance?
Where will its daring impudence find limits?
If human villainy and human life
shall wax in due proportion, if the son
shall always grow in wickedness past his father
the Gods must add another world to this
that all the sinners may have space enough.

Look at this man! He was my son and he
dishonours my wife's bed! By the dead's testimony
he's clearly proved the vilest, falsest wretch.
Come,—you could stain your conscience with the im-
    purity,—
show me your face; show it to me, your father.

You are the veritable holy man!
You walked with Gods in chastity immaculate!

I'll not believe your boasts of Gods' companionship:
the Gods are not so simple nor so ignorant.
Go, boast that you eat no meat, that you have Orpheus
for your king. Read until you are demented
your great thick books whose substance is as smoke.
For I have found you out. I tell you all,
avoid such men as he. They hunt their prey
with holy-seeming words, but their designs
are black and ugly. "She is dead" you thought,
"and that will save me." Fool, it is chiefly that
which proves your guilt. What oath that you can swear,
what speech that you can make for your acquittal
outweighs this letter of hers? You'll say, to be sure,
she was your enemy and that the bastard son
is always hateful to the legitimate line.
Your words would argue her a foolish merchant
whose stock of merchandise was her own life
if she should throw away what she held dearest
to gratify her enmity for you.

Or you will tell me that this frantic folly
is inborn in a woman's nature; man
is different: but I know that young men
are no more to be trusted than a woman
when love disturbs the youthful blood in them.
The very male in them will make them false.
But why should I debate against you in words?
Here is the dead, surest of witnesses.
Get from this land with all the speed you can
to exile,—may you rot there! Never again
come to our city, God-built Athens, nor
to countries over which my spear is king.

If I should take this injury at your hands
and pardon you, then Sinis of the Isthmus
whom once I killed would vow I never killed him,
but only bragged of the deed. And Sciron's rocks
washed by the sea would call me liar when
I swore I was a terror to ill-doers.

CHORUS LEADER

I cannot say of any man: he is happy.
See here how former happiness lies uprooted!

HIPPOLYTUS

Your mind and intellect are subtle, father:
here you have a subject dressed in eloquent words;
but if you lay the matter bare of words
the matter is not eloquent. I am
no man to speak with vapid, precious skill
before a mob, although among my equals
and in a narrow circle I am held
not unaccomplished in the eloquent art.
That is as it should be. The demagogue
who charms a crowd is scorned by cultured experts.
But here in this necessity I must speak.
First I shall take the argument you first
urged as so irrefutable and deadly.
You see the earth and air about you, father?
In all of that there lives no man more chaste
than I, though you deny it.
It is my rule to honour the Gods first
and then to have as friends only such men
as do no sin, nor offer wicked service
nor will consent to sin to serve a friend
as a return for kindness. I am no railer
at my companions. Those who are my friends
find me as much their friends when they are absent
as when we are together.

There is one thing that I have never done, the thing
of which you think that you convict me, father,
I am a virgin to this very day.
Save what I have heard or what I have seen in pictures
I'm ignorant of the deed. Nor do I wish
to see such things for I've a maiden soul.
But say you disbelieve my chastity.
Then tell me how it was *your* wife seduced me:

was it because she was more beautiful
than all the other women in the world?
Or did I think, when I had taken her,
to win your place and kingdom for a dowry
and live in your own house? I would have been
a fool, a senseless fool, if I had dreamed it.
Was rule so sweet? Never, I tell you, Theseus,
for the wise. A man whom power has so enchanted
must be demented. I would wish to be
first in the contests of the Hellenic Games
but in the city I'd take second place
and an enduring happy life among
the best society who are my friends.
So one has time to work and danger's absence
has charms above the royal diadem.
But a word more and my defence is finished.
If I had one more witness to my character,
if I were tried when *she* still saw the light,
deeds would have helped you as you scanned your friends
to know the true from the false. But now I swear,
I swear to you by Zeus, the God of oaths,
by this deep rooted fundament of earth,
I never sinned against you with your wife
nor would have wished or thought of it.
If I have been a villain may I die
unfamed, unknown, a homeless stateless beggar,
an exile! May the earth and sea refuse
to give my body rest when I am dead!
Whether your wife took her own life because
she was afraid, I do not know. I may not speak
further than this.
Virtuous she was in deed although not virtuous:
I that have virtue used it to my ruin.

CHORUS LEADER

You have rebutted the charge enough by your oath:
it is a great pledge you took in the God's name.

THESEUS

Why, here's a spell-binding magician for you!
He wrongs his father and then trusts his craft,
his smooth beguiling craft to lull my anger.

HIPPOLYTUS

Father, I must wonder at this in you.
If I were father now, and you were son,
I would not have banished you to exile! I
would have killed you if I thought you touched my wife.

THESEUS

This speech is worthy of you: but you'll not die so.
You'll not prescribe your martyrdom to me.
A quick death is the easiest of ends
for miserable men. No, you'll go wandering
far from your fatherland and beg your way.
This is the payment of the impious man.

HIPPOLYTUS

What will you do? You will not wait until
time's pointing finger proves me innocent.
Must I go at once to banishment?

THESEUS

                    Yes, and had I the power,
your place of banishment would be beyond
the limits of the world, the encircling sea
and the Atlantic Pillars.
That is the measure of my hate, my son.

HIPPOLYTUS

Pledges, oaths and oracles,—you will not test them?
You will banish me from the kingdom without trial?

THESEUS

This letter here is proof without lot-casting.
The ominous birds may fly above my head:
they do not trouble me.

HIPPOLYTUS
                    Eternal Gods!
Dare I speak out, since I am ruined now
through loyalty to the oath I took by you?
No, he would not believe who should believe
and I should be false to my oath for nothing.

THESEUS

This is more of your holy juggling!
I cannot stomach it. Away with you!
Get from this country,—and go quickly!

HIPPOLYTUS

Where shall I turn? What friend will take me in,
when I am banished on a charge like this?

THESEUS

Doubtless some man who loves to entertain
his wife's seducers welcoming them at the hearth.

HIPPOLYTUS

That blow went home.
I am near crying when I think that I
am judged to be guilty and that it is you who are judge.

THESEUS

You might have sobbed and snivelled long ago,
and thought of that before when you resolved
to rape your father's wife.

HIPPOLYTUS

                    House, speak for me!
Take voice and bear me witness if I have sinned.

THESEUS

You have a clever trick of citing witnesses,
Whose testimony is dumb. Here is your handiwork

(*pointing to the body.*)

It, too, can't speak,—but it convicts you.

HIPPOLYTUS

If I could only find
another *me* to look me in the face
and see my tears and all that I am suffering!

THESEUS

Yes, in self-worship you are certainly practised.
You are more at home there than in the other virtues,
justice, for instance, and duty towards a father.

HIPPOLYTUS

Unhappy mother mine, and bitter birth-pangs,
when you gave me to the world! I would not wish
on any of my friends a bastard's birth.

THESEUS (*to the servants*)

Drag him away!
Did you not hear me, men, a long time since
proclaiming his decree of banishment?

HIPPOLYTUS

Let one of them touch me at his peril! But you,
you drive me out yourself,—if you have the heart!

THESEUS

I'll do it, too, unless you go at once.
No, there is no chance that pity for your exile
will steal on my hard heart and make me change.

(*Theseus goes out.*)

HIPPOLYTUS

So, I'm condemned and there is no release.
I know the truth and dare not tell the truth.

(*He turns to the statue of Artemis.*)

Daughter of Leto, dearest of the Gods to me,
comrade and partner in the hunt, behold me,
banished from famous Athens.

Farewell, city! Farewell Erectheus' land!
Troezen, farewell! I had a happy boyhood
in your flat plains.
This is the last time I shall look upon you,
the last time I shall greet you.

(*To his companions.*)

Come friends, you are of my age and of this country,
say your farewells and set me on my way
you will not see a man more innocent,—
innocent despite my judge!—condemned to banishment.

CHORUS
   Strophe
The care of God for us is a great thing,
if a man believe it at heart:
it plucks the burden of sorrow from him.
So I have a secret hope
of someone, a God, who is wise and plans
but my hopes grow dim when I see
the deeds of men and their destinies.

For fortune is ever veering, and the currents of life are shifting
shifting, wandering for ever.

   Antistrophe
This is the lot in life I seek
and I pray that God may grant it me,
luck and prosperity,
and a heart untroubled by anguish.
And a mind that is neither false clipped coin,
nor too clear eyed in sincerity,
that I may lightly change my ways,
my ways of to-day when to-morrow comes,
and so be happy all my life long.

   Strophe
My heart is no longer clear:
I have seen what I never dreamed,

I have seen the brightest star of Athens,
stricken by a father's wrath,
banished to an alien land.

Sands of the sea-shore!
Thicket of the mountain!
Where with his pacing hounds
he hunted wild beasts and killed
to the honour of holy Dictynna.

Antistrophe

He will never again mount his car
with its span of Venetian mares,
nor fill the ring of Limnae with the sound of horses' hoofs.
The music which never slept
on the strings of his lyre, shall be dumb,
shall be dumb in his father's house.
The haunts of the Goddess Maid
in the deep rich meadow shall want their crowns.
You are banished: there's an end
of the rivalry of maids for your love.

Epode

But my sorrow shall not die
still my eyes shall be wet with tears
for your heartless doom.
Sad mother, you bore him in vain:
I am angry against the Gods.
Sister Graces, why did you let him go
guiltless, out of his native land,
out of his father's house?

Scene VI

(*Enter a Messenger, one of Hippolytus' Comrades.*)

MESSENGER

Where shall I go to find King Theseus, women?
If you know, tell me. Is he within doors?

CHORUS
Here he is coming out.

MESSENGER
King Theseus,
I bring you news worthy of much thought
for you and all the citizens who live
in Athens' walls and boundaries of Troezen.

THESEUS
What is it? Has some still newer disaster
Seized on the citizens of both my cities?

MESSENGER
Hippolytus is dead: I may almost say dead:
he sees the light of day still, though the balance
that holds him in this world is slight indeed.

THESEUS
Who killed him? I can guess that someone hated him,
whose wife he raped, as he did mine, his father's.

MESSENGER
It was the horses of his own car that killed him,
they, and the curses of your lips,
the curses you invoked against your son,
and prayed the Lord of Ocean to fulfil them.

THESEUS
O Gods,—Poseidon, you are then truly
my father! You have heard my prayers.
How did he die? Tell me. How did the beam
of Justice's dead-fall strike him, my dishonourer?

MESSENGER
We were combing our horses' coats beside the sea,
where the waves came crashing to the shore. And we were
    crying
for one had come and told us that our master,
Hippolytus should walk this land no more,

since you had laid hard banishment upon him.
Then he came himself down to the shore to us,
with the same refrain of tears,
and with him walked a countless company
of friends and young men his own age.

But at last he gave over crying and said:
Why do I rave like this? It is my father
who has commanded and I must obey him.
Prepare my horses, men, and harness them.
This is no longer a city of mine.
Then every man made haste. Before you could say the
    words,
there was the chariot ready before our master.
He put his feet into the driver's rings,
and took the reins from the rail into his hands.
But first he folded his hands like this and prayed:
Zeus, let me die now, if I have been guilty!
Let my father know that he has done me wrong,
whether I live to see the day or not.

With that, he took the goad and touched the horses.
And we his servants followed our master's car,
close by the horses' heads, on the straight road
that leads to Argos and to Epidaurus.
When we were entering the lonely country
the other side of the border, where the shore
goes down to the Saronic Gulf, a rumbling
deep in the earth, terrible to hear,
growled like the thunder of Father Zeus.
The horses raised their heads, pricked up their ears,
and gusty fear was on us all to know,
whence came the sound. As we looked towards the shore,
where the waves were beating, we saw a wave appear,
a miracle wave, lifting its crest to the sky,
so high that Sciron's coast was blotted out
from my eye's vision. And it hid the Isthmus
and the Asclepius Rock. To the shore it came,
swelling, boiling, crashing, casting its surf around,

to where the chariot stood.
But at the very moment when it broke,
the wave threw up a monstrous savage bull.
Its bellowing filled the land, and the land echoed it,
with shuddering emphasis. And sudden panic
fell on the horses in the car. But the master,—
he was used to horses' ways,—all his life long
he had been with horses—took a firm grip of the reins
and lashed the ends behind his back and pulled
like a sailor at the oar. The horses bolted:
their teeth were clenched upon the fire-forged bit.
They heeded neither the driver's hand nor harness
nor the jointed car. As often as he would turn them
with guiding hand to the soft sand of the shore,
the bull appeared in front to head them off,
maddening the team with terror.
But when in frenzy they charged towards the cliffs,
the bull came galloping beside the rail,
silently following until he brought disaster,
capsizing the car, striking the wheel on a rock.
Then all was in confusion. Axles of wheels,
and lynch-pins flew up into the air,
and he the unlucky driver, tangled in the reins,
was dragged along in an inextricable
knot and his dear head pounded on the rocks,
his body bruised. He cried aloud and terrible
his voice rang in our ears: Stand, horses, stand!
You were fed in my stables. Do not kill me!
My father's curse! His curse! Will none of you
save me? I am innocent. Save me!

Many of us had will enough, but all
were left behind in the race. Getting free of the reins
somehow he fell. There was still life in him.
But the horses vanished and that ill-omened monster,
somewhere, I know not where, in the rough cliffs.

I am only a slave in your household, King Theseus,
but I shall never be able to believe

that your son was guilty, not though the tribe of women
were hanged for it, not though the weight of tablets
of a high pine of Ida, filled with writing,
accused him,—for I know that he was good.

CHORUS LEADER

It has been fulfilled, this bitter, new disaster,
for what is doomed and fated there is no quittance.

THESEUS

For hatred of the sufferer I was glad
at what you told me. Still, he was my son.
God sanctioned the tie which bound us and I reverence it.
I neither rejoice nor sorrow at this thing.

MESSENGER

What is your pleasure that we do with him?
Would you have him brought to you? If I might counsel,
you would not be harsh with your son,—for he is dying.

THESEUS

Bring him to me that I may see his face.
He swore that he had never wronged my wife.
I will refute him with God's punishing stroke.

CHORUS

Cypris, you guide men's hearts
and the inflexible
hearts of the Gods and with you
comes Love with the flashing wings,
comes Love with the swiftest of wings.
Over the earth he flies
and the loud-echoing salt-sea.
He bewitches and maddens the heart
of the victim he swoops upon.
He bewitches the race of the mountain haunting
lions and beasts of the sea,
and all the creatures that earth feeds,
and the blazing sun sees,—

and man, too,—
over all you hold kingly power,
Love, you are only ruler
over all these.

Epilogue

ARTEMIS

I call on the noble king, the son of Aegeus,
to hear me! It is I, Artemis, child of Leto.

Miserable man, what joy have you in this?
you have murdered a son, you have broken nature's laws.
Dark indeed was the conclusion
you drew from your wife's lying accusations,
but plain for all to see is the destruction
to which they led you.
There is a hell beneath the earth: haste to it,
and hide your head there! Or will you take wings,
and choosing the life of a bird instead of man
keep your feet from destruction's path in which they tread?
Amongst good men, at least, you have no share in life.
Hear me tell you, Theseus, how these things came to pass.
I shall not better them, but I will give you pain.
I have come here for this,—to show you that your son's heart
was always just, so just that for his good name
he endured to die. I will show you, too,
the frenzied love that seized your wife, or I may call it,
a noble innocence. For that most hated Goddess,
hated by all of us whose joy is virginity,
drove her with love's sharp prickings to desire
your son. She tried to overcome her love
with the mind's power, but at last against her will,
she fell by the nurse's stratagems,
the nurse, who told your son under oath her mistress loved
    him.
But he, just man, did not fall in with her
counsels, and even when reviled by you
refused to break the oath he had pledged.
Such was his piety. But your wife fearing

lest she be proved the sinner wrote a letter,
a letter full of lies; and so she killed
your son by treachery; but she convinced you.

THESEUS
Alas!

ARTEMIS
This is a bitter story, Theseus. Stay,
hear more that you may groan the more.
You know you had three curses from your father,
three, clear for you to use? One you have launched,
vile wretch, at your own son, when you might have
spent it upon an enemy. Your father,
King of the Sea, in lovingkindness to you
gave you, by his bequest, all that he ought.
But you've been proved at fault both in his eyes
and mine in that you did not stay for oaths
nor voice of oracles, nor gave a thought
to what time might have shown; only too quickly
you hurled the curses at your son and killed him.

THESEUS
Mistress, I am destroyed.

ARTEMIS
You have sinned indeed, but yet you may win pardon.
For it was Cypris managed the thing this way
to gratify her anger against Hippolytus.
You know there is an understanding among the Gods.
No one may fly in the face of another's wish:
we remain aloof and neutral. Else, I assure you,
had I not feared Zeus, I never would have endured
such shame as this,—my best friend among men
killed, and I could do nothing.
As for you, in the first place ignorance acquits you,
and then your wife, by her death, destroyed the proofs
the verbal proofs which might have still convinced you.
You and I are the chief sufferers, Theseus.

Misfortune for you, grief for me.
The Gods do not rejoice when pious worshippers die:
the wicked we destroy, children, house and all.

CHORUS

Here comes the suffering Hippolytus,
his fair young body and his golden head,
a battered wreck. O trouble of the house,
what double sorrow from the hand of God
has been fulfilled for this our royal palace!

HIPPOLYTUS

A battered wreck of body! Unjust father,
and oracle unjust,—this is your work.
Woe for my fate!
My head is filled with shooting agony,
and in my brain there is a leaping fire.
Let me be!
For I would rest my weary frame awhile.
Curse on my team! How often have I fed you
from my own hand, you who have murdered me!
O, O!
In God's name touch my wounded body gently.
Who is this standing on the right of me?
Come lift me carefully, bear me easily,
a man unlucky, cursed by my own father
in bitter error. Zeus, do you see this,
see me that worshipped God in piety,
me that excelled all men in chastity,
see me now go to death which gapes before me;
all my life lost, and all for nothing now
labours of piety in the face of men?

O the pain, the pain that comes upon me!
Let me be, let me be, you wretches!
May death the healer come for me at last!
You kill me ten times over with this pain.
O for a spear with a keen cutting edge
to shear me apart,—and give me my last sleep!

Father, your deadly curse!
This evil comes from some manslaying of old,
some ancient tale of murder among my kin.
But why should it strike me who am clear of guilt?
What is there to say? How can I shake from me
this pitiless pain? O death, black night of death,
resistless death, come to me now the miserable,
and give me sleep!

ARTEMIS

Unhappy boy! You are yoked to a cruel fate.
The nobility of your soul has proved your ruin.

HIPPOLYTUS

O divine fragrance! Even in my pain
I sense it, and the suffering is lightened.
The Goddess Artemis is near this place.

ARTEMIS

She is, the dearest of the Gods to you.

HIPPOLYTUS

You see my suffering, mistress?

ARTEMIS

I see it. Heavenly law forbids my tears.

HIPPOLYTUS

Gone is your huntsman, gone your servant now.

ARTEMIS

Yes, truly: but you die beloved by me.

HIPPOLYTUS

Gone is your groom, gone your shrine's guardian.

ARTEMIS

Cypris, the worker of mischief, so contrived.

HIPPOLYTUS

Alas, I know the Goddess who destroyed me!

ARTEMIS

She blamed your disrespect, hated your chastity.

HIPPOLYTUS

She claimed us three as victims then, did Cypris?

ARTEMIS

Your father, you and me to make a third.

HIPPOLYTUS

Yes, I am sorry for my father's suffering.

ARTEMIS

Cypris deceived him by her cunning snares.

HIPPOLYTUS

O father, this is sorrow for you indeed!

THESEUS

I, too, am dead now. I have no more joy in life.

HIPPOLYTUS

I sorrow for you in this more than myself.

THESEUS

Would that it was I who was dying instead of you!

HIPPOLYTUS

Bitter were Poseidon's gifts, my father, bitter.

THESEUS

Would that they had never come into my mouth.

HIPPOLYTUS

Even without them, you would have killed me,—
you were so angry.

THESEUS

      A God tripped up my judgment.

HIPPOLYTUS

O, if only men might be a curse to Gods!

ARTEMIS

Hush, that is enough! You shall not be unavenged,
Cypris shall find the angry shafts she hurled
against you for your piety and innocence
shall cost her dear.
I'll wait until she loves a mortal next time,
and with this hand,—with these unerring arrows
I'll punish him.

To you, unfortunate Hippolytus,
by way of compensation for these ills,
I will give the greatest honours of Troezen.
Unwedded maids before the day of marriage
will cut their hair in your honour. You will reap
through the long cycle of time, a rich reward in tears.
And when young girls sing songs they will not forget you,
your name will not be left unmentioned,
nor Phaedra's love for you remain unsung.

        (To Theseus.)

Son of old Aegeus, take your son
to your embrace. Draw him to you. Unknowing
you killed him. It is natural for men
to err when they are blinded by the Gods.

        (To Hippolytus.)

Do not bear a grudge against your father.
It was fate that you should die so.
Farewell, I must not look upon the dead.
My eye must not be polluted by the last
gaspings for breath. I see you are near this.

HIPPOLYTUS

Farewell to you too, holy maiden! Go in peace.
You can lightly leave a long companionship.
You bid me end my quarrel with my father,
and I obey. In the past too I obeyed you.

The darkness is upon my eyes already.

Father, lay hold on me and lift me up.

THESEUS

Alas, what are you doing to me, my son?

HIPPOLYTUS

I am dying. I can see the gates of death.

THESEUS

And so you leave me, my hands stained with murder.

HIPPOLYTUS

No, for I free you from all guilt in this.

THESEUS

You will acquit me of blood guiltiness?

HIPPOLYTUS

So help me Artemis of the conquering bow!

THESEUS

Dear son, how noble you have proved to me!

HIPPOLYTUS

Yes, pray to heaven for such legitimate sons.

THESEUS

Woe for your goodness, piety and virtue.

HIPPOLYTUS

Farewell to you, too, father, a long farewell!

THESEUS

Dear son, bear up. Do not forsake me.

HIPPOLYTUS

This is the end of what I have to bear.
I'm gone. Cover my face up quickly.

THESEUS

Pallas Athene's famous city,
What a man you have lost! Alas for me!
Cypris, how many of your injuries
I shall remember.

CHORUS

This is a common grief for all the city;
it came unlooked for. There shall be
a storm of multitudinous tears for this;
the lamentable stories of great men
prevail more than of humble folk.